Rodney Loeppky
A Deal They Can't Resist

I0103791

De Gruyter Contemporary Social Sciences

Volume 7

Rodney Loeppky

A Deal They Can't Resist

Adaptive Accumulation and American Public Policy

DE GRUYTER

ISBN 978-3-11-154083-2
e-ISBN (PDF) 978-3-11-076180-1
e-ISBN (EPUB) 978-3-11-076185-6
ISSN 2747-5689
e-ISSN 2747-5697

Library of Congress Control Number: 2021947924

Bibliographic information published by the Deutsche Nationalbibliothek
The Deutsche Nationalbibliothek lists this publication in the Deutsche Nationalbibliografie;
detailed bibliographic data are available on the Internet at http://dnb.dnb.de.

© 2024 Walter de Gruyter GmbH, Berlin/Boston
This volume is text- and page-identical with the hardback published in 2022.
Cover image: Nigel Stripe / iStock / Getty Images Plus (stethoscope)
BrianAJackson / iStock / Getty Images Plus (doctoral cap)

www.degruyter.com

Contents

Chapter 1: Introduction

The study of America is the scrutiny of contradictions. It is, after all, a place where unparalleled wealth is accompanied by extensive, grinding poverty. Where else do we find the most advanced biomedical and health establishment in the world, matched by the exclusion of tens of millions from healthcare? It is a society with a reverence for individual rights and freedoms, but one which has also fostered the largest *per capita* prison population in the world. Indeed, in the land of ostensible equality and opportunity, the extent of class, race, and gender inequalities often feels overwhelming. Some have argued that these social incongruities signal a decaying society, possibly even the decline of a US empire, not dissimilar from the corrosive dynamics that extinguished ancient Rome or allowed the sun to set on the British Empire (Wood, 2004; Ferguson, 2005; Greer, 2014).

Americans, however, have neither viewed themselves with such grandeur nor understood themselves operating within any predictable pattern of history. On the contrary, a revolutionary historical narrative pervades American political culture, with 'exceptionalism' remaining a constant refrain. The special brand of US democracy and its faith in human progress, the capitalist marketplace, and the individual will, ultimately, are thought to overcome all challenges. Most political economists and social theorists, of course, have viewed this proposition with skepticism, focusing their criticism on the specificity of US capitalism, with its strong neoliberal characteristics and grossly unequal social outcomes. Nowhere in the capitalist world have the extensions of the free market been as great as they have in the United States, where Nancy Fraser (2019) has argued that the post-Reagan battle between reactionary neoliberals (Republican-led) and progressive neoliberals (Democrat-led) has resulted in the hyper-reactionary neoliberal brand of the Trump administration.

> The political universe that Trump upended was highly restrictive. It was built around the opposition between two versions of neoliberalism, distinguished chiefly on the axis of recognition. Granted, one could choose between multiculturalism and ethnonationalism. But one was stuck, either way, with financialization and deindustrialization. With the menu limited to *progressive* and *reactionary neoliberalism*, there was no force to oppose the decimation of working-class and middle-class standards of living. Anti-neoliberal projects were severely marginalized, if not simply excluded, from the public sphere (2019, p. 18).

This is not to say that neoliberal capitalism in the U.S. proceeds in a completely unfettered fashion—US capital is subject to state regulation (both federal and state), just like everywhere else in the world. But US political culture validates

https://doi.org/10.1515/9783110761801-001

market competition across societal activities that are viewed elsewhere as inherently public—from postal service to post-secondary education, from healthcare to incarceration. Even in its willingness to project military power abroad, political economists see the maintenance of an 'empire of capital', prying open societies to better accommodate the free movement of (especially US) capital (Wood, 2002).

Why should any of this come as a surprise? After all, this has long been the age of neoliberalism, the history of which puts the Anglo-American world at the cutting edge. The pedigree is difficult to deny: from the Reagan and Thatcher revolutions, through 'third way' Clintonians and Blairites, and on to the full-blown neoliberal fury of the Trump and Johnson administrations. Neoliberalism in Anglo-American countries is said to be more than just the uptake of classical liberal principles—rather, it is the unwavering disavowal of all things Keynesian and the systematic dismantling of the institutions of post-war society (Peet, 2003). At the same time, however, more than a whiff of hypocrisy is notable here, because this disavowal only seems to hold while capitalism is bullish in nature. Whenever prospects for economic growth slow—the Savings & Loan Crisis, Black Monday, the 2008 financial crisis, or the COVID 19 shutdown—even the starkest free market advocates in Congress and elsewhere willingly endorse multi-billion or trillion-dollar government interventions.

This book interrogates, beyond such bailouts, whether the 'unbridled' brand of US neoliberalism, in fact, always holds true. Certainly, the financial crises listed above demonstrate an especially free ranging financial market, with a good deal of industry-friendly regulatory oversight. In that arena, it could be said that the state has, intermittently, receded from view, allowing a much wider, unsupervised ambit of corporate activity. And one would be correct for sensing a more general 'retreat of the state' across a wide array of activities, as the specter of 'privatization' seems ubiquitous at all levels of government. It has been estimated, in fact, that of the $6 trillion in government spending across the U.S., at least a full $1 trillion now goes to private companies (Ball, 2014). A large part of that privatization dynamic, however, does not suggest the standard image of government 'getting out of the way'. This work maintains that there has been a large-scale movement of capital into central public policy domains, where government retains and even builds on its dominant functions. More specifically, it argues that part of the development of US neoliberalism involves *adaptive accumulation*, a process in which capital allies or aligns itself with public objectives and institutions, as a means to transform or reroute public revenues into private profit streams. Along the way, corporate organizations 'adapt' their roles as pure market actors, taking up and inhabiting quasi-public aspirations as a central part of their commercial mission. The state, in all its complexities, proceeds with this relationship, as it both addresses budgetary dilemmas brought on by regular rounds of austerity and extends or carves out new areas of accumulative growth for corporate America.

The sectors involved range in scope and magnitude, from substantial to enormous, but the present work does not presume to capture every manifestation of this process. Instead, it gives an indicative account of concrete cases that challenges our sense of a hyper-neoliberal US political economy, where the 'rules of reproduction' are not as self-evident as we might assume. Samuel Knafo and Benno Teschke (2020) have made the argument that when we examine historically specific cases of capitalist development, it is imperative that we not read the nature or outcome of their development from some inherent attributes of capitalism. In the authors' words, there is a necessity to avoid, "a fetishized conception," where "[what] is conceptually rendered as an auto-generative logic of action grates with the historical tracking of capitalism ... as a contested and concrete process" (2020, p. 77). The authors seek "to open up space for re-thinking capitalism as a historically open rather than theoretically-closed category" (2020, p. 77). The utilization of adaptive accumulation to view the specific nature of US political economy demands this same historically open perspective. It requires that we consider the existence of a symbiotic relationship between state and capital across a range of significant economic sectors, potentially, *as a constitutive part* of American neoliberal development.

In order to make this argument, the work examines four separate arenas of public policy—military, healthcare, education and incarceration—as cases in which adaptive accumulation has taken hold. Taken together, these sectors make up a very large portion of public and private spending and, as such, represent a large share of US economic activity. Cobbling together estimates from only K-12 education, health, and incarceration, total government spending in these areas amounted to almost $5 trillion in 2019 (Wagner and Rabuy, 2017; Martin *et al.*, 2021; Hanson, no date). Potentially, this reveals two possibilities with respect to US political economy. The first, obviously, is that sectors of such size exhibit a broad appeal for those seeking profit streams, as room to transform public spending through adaptive accumulation remains extensive. Second, and more important, it might be fair to say that US economic strength is as reliant on these publicly-funded sectors as it is on the vitality of either its domestic consumption of goods or its financial sector. This is significant, because within political economy, much of the sectoral spending involved would be categorized as 'unproductive' components of economic activity. The implication is clear: in the heartland of neoliberal capitalism, publicly-funded sectors actually constitute one of the *differentia specifica* that drives American capitalist development. Rather than seeing them as either marginal attempts to 'shore up' capitalism or bloated government spending, it might be better to understand them as concrete specificities, integral to the US capitalist engine.

Before getting to these sectors, however, the second chapter provides the basic outlines for adaptive accumulation as an interpretive lens. With the strategic aim of readability, the chapter has been deliberately limited in size and conceptual scope. Those looking for a long, meandering, or overly abstract survey of literature on the state and political economy, or a 'deep dive' into value theory and accumulation, will have to look elsewhere. The point here is to specify the context of US neoliberalism, from which questions concerning the unique form of US capitalist practices emerge. From this, the chapter positions adaptive accumulation within a more critical set of perspectives on institutions, and it sets out the various functions that such accumulation serves its participant social actors. Ultimately, the objective is an enhanced understanding of neoliberalism, where we gain both a different version of 'privatization' and a more nuanced view of what the public realm means for corporate actors.

The third chapter proceeds to an examination of the public policy sector in which talk of state-supported capitalism all began: the military. Readers are, no doubt, more than familiar with the notion of a 'military-industrial complex', and it is the contemporary widespread application of that concept to other sectors that motivates a re-examination of neoliberalism in the American context. Logically, then, the work begins by examining the potential for adaptive accumulation in US military matters. Importantly, the chapter goes beyond weapons procurement issues usually involved in such discussions, as they have been both well explored elsewhere and are not especially indicative of adaptive accumulation. Instead, it highlights the more recent ways in which US military policy—as a form of public policy—has redirected societal revenues into private profit streams. This is a public policy process specific to the neoliberal era, and it demonstrates the manner in which corporate actors have been 'drafted' into public objectives, all with an eye to maintaining forward deployment capacities and an increasingly expensive high-tech arsenal in the context of an uncertain post-Cold War budgetary environment.

Following this, chapter four explores the domain that is often cited as the only serious rival to defense spending: health and healthcare. Health constitutes an immense area of activity, in which government involvement has grown, even while the U.S. remains the leading case of free market health delivery worldwide. Here, the argument is made that across several government-run or -regulated healthcare structures, from Medicare to so-called healthcare exchanges, corporations have been able to insert private forms of healthcare purchasing and provision, supported by government payments and subsidies. It is well known that US spending in health is typically twice as expensive as it is among its advanced industrial counterparts, even as the latter systems tend to be far more universalized and generous in their provisioning. The segmented nature of the US system, with very uneven but generous government involvement, makes this terrain particularly lucrative for capital. Cloaked in a shawl of concern for patients' well-being, health related corporations pursue a government-expanded terrain of public spending that carefully avoids the price restricting chokehold of universality. In the face of adaptive accumulation, it is little wonder that when 'Medicare For All' rose as a meaningful possibility (along with Bernie Sanders' campaign in late Fall 2019), the concerted and interest-laden denunciation of its 'fairness' and 'feasibility' was deafening.

Chapter five furthers this exploration into social policy, with an examination of education, where everything from programs like No Child Left Behind to the vast private systems of post-secondary institutions are open to scrutiny. Limiting its scope, however, the chapter considers the transformation of K-12 education, with its attendant connection to the charter school movement. The struggle around school transformation has been part of a process underway since the Reagan administration—designating 'crisis' in the public school system and identifying 'lost' schools and districts for conversion to 'free' charter organizations, a growing portion of which are for-profit or market-disciplined. Alongside the relentless, localized push towards charterization and marketization, federal and state legislation has cooperated with the standardization of curriculum, supplying a quantification of performance standards that has generated a lucrative parallel industry of tests, teaching materials and supplemental tutoring. As with other forms of inequality, this conversion process is directed predominantly at marginalized communities, where 'failing schools' come about as a result of grossly depleted resources. This creates a self-fulfilling reality, whereby under resourced, minority-populated public schools require 'rescuing' from the ostensible ineptitude of public management, clearing the ground for new forms of service delivery. Alarmingly, however, the evidence points to little or no progress with experimentation, unless union-busting of teachers, unequal access and redlining of performance results is considered progress.

The race-infused elements of this political economy are further highlighted within chapter six, an examination of the changing US incarceration system. The scene set here is not a happy one, with a post-1980 political agenda that has backed the execution of racist drug policies, 'three strikes' laws, and mandatory sentencing guidelines. The end result is the largest prison population in the world, with a grossly disproportionate black and Latino majority. In this context, the private incarceration industry has grown at both the federal and state level, providing fixed contracts based on per prisoner service payments. The grim public function fulfilled by these companies has proven lucrative, and the consequences for prison populations, by all reports, are not good. In short, if corrections and rehabilitation are the public function of federal and state prisons, the entry of private actors complicates this with perverse dual imperatives to increase prisoners and control costs, leading to less than humane conditions. None of this is made less complicated by the recurring detainment of immigrants, an additional and enticing field of profit for prison corporations, with less onerous regulations around standards than state or federal correction facilities. Operating a majority of detainment facilities in this area, private corporations have benefitted from successive administration policies that have subjected immigrants to 'securitized' and increasingly punitive conditions.

Overall, these cases render a picture that complicates our image of US political economy as the archetype of neoliberalism. This is not to suggest that US capitalism is now entirely state-led capitalism. On the contrary, it points towards an interpretation of capitalist development that begins from concrete historical circumstances. It cautions us from too quickly drawing the conclusion that problems associated with these sectors—high costs, poor quality control, dangerous outcomes, and stepped-up racism—are merely the neoliberal product of state retreat, combined with an increasingly unbound market. Consistently, the circumstances of adaptive accumulation are more complicated. Instead, the state plays a co-active role in carving out niche areas of service delivery, or it intervenes to shore up an existing area of provision. Corporate actors, new and old, struggle politically to participate in this largesse, but they also do so with full cognizance of their new public persona. Whether this is draped in the patriotism necessary for military service contracts, or the compassionate endeavor to preserve the health and well-being of US citizens, this new pseudo-public character offers a valuable shield from political criticism and, often, economic competition. And, as we will see in the ensuing chapters, this is a part of the problem—the delivery of public objectives by private actors often leads to suboptimal results, but policymakers see no choice once these systems are in place. The challenge for scholars and practitioners alike, one taken up by this work, is to determine the degree to which this embedded position of private actors is both a permanent and constitutive element in the American political economy.

Chapter 2: Adaptive Accumulation: Public Objectives, Private Revenues

In the study of political economy, the debate concerning the role of the state in capitalist accumulation has proven to be enduring. For theoretical *aficionados*, the well-known Miliband-Poulantzas debate, along with its ensuing derivative discussions, constitute a landmark in the understanding of the state's relationship with capitalism, but has still not resulted in settled and agreed-upon conclusions (Poulantzas, 1969; Miliband, 1970; Panitch, 1999; Jessop, 2008). The state-capital relationship can take varied form over time, and it also varies by geographic region. As such, rather than an over-generalizing set of assertions, the more modest theoretical ambitions in this chapter pertain to a particular set of contemporary dynamics in the United States, providing an updated elaboration of US political economy and neoliberalism. It is not an attempt to 're-invent the wheel' or claim that all hitherto political economy has somehow 'got it wrong'. The aim is to highlight the shape of and motivations for *adaptive accumulation* as a significant factor within American neoliberalism, and its scope is not intended to explain every element of US political economy. Readers seeking a comprehensive theoretical exposition—i.e. in search of sweeping conceptual and historical axioms—are recommended to look elsewhere. Intentionally brief in reach, the chapter seeks to clarify a singular dynamic that the empirical cases of this book hold in common—the sustained and strategic entry of private capital in government-run US programs.

On the face of it, such an update might seem unnecessary. The prevailing characterization of US political economy as uniquely Anglo-American could be understood as sufficient to capture the most important components of the state-capital relationship. By this characterization, the state is understood to be minimalist or subordinated with regard to capitalist civil society. Institutionalist approaches, for instance, have emphasized the robust flexibility afforded to capital in the American context. From industrial relations to investment regimes, from regulatory leniency to banking permissiveness, capital enjoys considerable maneuverability in the U.S., which it is said to lack in most other advanced industrial countries. There is no doubt that 'competitive advantage' has been sought by many countries by way of regulatory and institutional permissiveness, but the US state has proven malleable in ways that offers comparatively more flexibility for capital (Hollingsworth, 1997). Whether this flexibility and minimalism is subject to derision or celebration has depended on ideological disposition, as well as the time frame in which it has been considered. So-called shareholder capitalism in the U.S. has been lauded by institutionalists for its innovative and dynamic growth potential, but also mildly criticized for its correlation with instability and crisis orientation. Either way, the institutional depiction of US capitalism remains the same: a lean state, supporting a highly fluid accumulation environment, both in finance and production arenas.

From an expressly critical standpoint, Marxist political economy has also mixed the Anglo-American trajectory into its analysis of American neoliberalism. While capitalist social relations are understood in global terms, there is no doubt that the U.S. and the U.K. are taken as the states most disposed to capitalism as a social force. For instance, 'political Marxists' have emphasized Anglo-American accumulation patterns, which are said to differ historically from a European, continental tradition. This is rooted largely in the differing historical circumstances in which the transition to capitalism took hold in different parts of the world. Ellen Wood (1992), among others, has underlined the fact that capitalist production finds its origins in agricultural England, and that it is in England where it found its most unadulterated form. Whereas on the continent, centuries later, the introduction of capitalism emerges in lock step with directed state policies, capitalism in England had long since relegated the state to its most subservient form. It is within the latter political tradition that US society, from its earliest days, both embraced and developed petty agricultural production and, ultimately, the peculiar form of American capitalism, centered on a domestic market for consumable goods. As Wood (1992) has put it, both the UK and the US have been

> ... most responsive to the pure logic of capitalism and to the imperatives of mass consumer market. While other advanced industrial economies have more consistently utilized the instrumentalities of the state to enhance long-term market share, these two less adulterated capitalisms have been more susceptible to the demands of short term profits (1992, p. 106).

Whether from an institutionalist or Marxist standpoint, this categorization of American capitalism has merit, but it is surely important to avoid the temptation to view its outcomes as a historical necessity. In this sense, it is productive to situate historical state and institutional forms in the American neoliberal context, but this needs to be informed by the concrete specificities of the current era. Not surprisingly, then, critical streams of institutionalist and Marxist studies alike have called into question the necessity of viewing Anglo capitalisms through a pre-arranged lens. For instance, some in institutionalist circles have directly questioned the strict divide between liberal market economies (LMEs) and coordinated market economies (CMEs), a division that holds very consistently through much of the literature (Goodin, 2003; Howell, 2003). David Coates (2014) has argued that this division leads analysts to over-emphasize the more obvious differences, such as financial markets, industrial relations and labour relations. And in the case of the U.S., such analyses tend to evade

> ... the close working relationship between the Pentagon and the US engineering industry, between the oil industry and the Department of Energy, between large agribusinesses and the Agriculture Department, and between large pharmaceutical companies and federally funded basic research and Medicare/Medicaid spending (2014, p. 173).

Similarly, the LME category itself tends to be underexplored, and it is instead projected as simply lacking the fulsome public policy present in coordinated economies. The danger is that Anglo-American political economies are considered solely as, "a residual category ... mostly characterized in negative terms, that is, in terms of what they lack ... rather than analyzed in terms of alternative logic that animates them" (Thelen, quoted in Howell 2003, 107).

Marxists, in turn, have further questioned the utility of categories attached to historical institutionalism, and even those within Marxism itself. Greg Albo (2005) has forcefully questioned the degree to which institutionalists tend to reify the structures they seek to elucidate, attributing to them a determining effect. He points out that institutions possess a certain crystallized stability, but they are ultimately constraining or enabling rules which are continuously subject to power relations and social agents. Crucially, these "agents' conflicting strategies for reproduction continually transform and reorder these institutions" (2005, p. 80). This suggests far less rigidity in the manner in which the institutional structure of capitalism in any one region or country should be considered. In this sense, history must, ultimately, be viewed as open and not entirely beholden to the historical structure running from past to present.

It is important to consider public policy and policy outcomes not as mere 'predictables', but rather as dynamic outcomes of agents' actions in an institutional matrix subject to historical change. In contemporary capitalist social relations, then, this requires that we understand the strategies of agents of neoliberal social structure, as well as their constraints and capacities within the complex specificities of institutions and historical trajectory. Dennis Pilon (2015) has identified this practice, broadly, as 'critical institutionalism', suggesting that neoliberalism needs to be viewed simultaneously as the outcome of social structures that shape social behavior *and* institutional structures subject to change through social action. This means that "actors not only engage in action within a given institutional matrix but, in certain circumstances, can reflexively reconstitute institutions and their resulting matrix" (Jessop, 2001, p. 1226). Ultimately, we are left with a rendition of the contemporary period, in which the 'rules of reproduction' cannot be worked out from a predetermined institutional template. Instead, taking historical specificity more seriously should allow for the possibility of unexpected outcomes (Knafo and Teschke, 2020).

With this in mind, a particular problem emerges in relation to the U.S., insofar as the state takes on an accommodating but not-so-thin interventionist role. Amidst the talk of unbridled US capitalism, there are, across multiple sectors, increasing allusions to the existence of 'industrial complexes'. These suggestions, of course, harken back to the now legendary assertion by then President Dwight Eisenhower in his farewell address that a military-industrial complex had emerged in the United States. Eisenhower, concerned about alarming budgetary scenarios, warned that this complex was exercising "total influence—economic, political, even spiritual—[and] is felt in every city, every State house, every office of the Federal Government" (Fallows, 2002, p. 133). However, outside of associated concepts like 'revolving door' and 'iron triangles', the industrial complex remains a very elusive concept in political economy. While conjuring up images of a totalizing effort towards the industrial well-being of military producers, both the contours and politico-economic status of complexes remain hazy and conceptually immature, often easily associated with dismissible, conspiratorial thinking.

Nonetheless, the language of industrial complexes has become a popular touchstone, referencing sectoral juggernauts that exhibit undue—often negative—influence on production, price, distribution, and politics. As such, beyond references to military procurement, the arenas of health, incarceration and education have now emerged as popular examples of industrial complexes. The resilience of this terminology directly challenges notions of the American state-capital relationship as consistently minimalist and non-interventionist. To be sure, the claim here is not that the US state has somehow entirely spurned its facilitation of a leaner, more flexible form of capitalist accumulation—witness, for instance, the US financial arena, with its well-documented state deregulation, flurry of private transactions, and infusion of public money in the wake of catastrophic collapse (Henwood, 2011). But in other areas, the state maintains a regulatory mechanism that not only facilitates but utilizes the public domain—or a perception of the public domain—to buoy the accumulation potential of capital.

Heidi Gerstenberger (2011), for instance, has criticized both institutionalist and Marxist literature for conceptually neglecting some obviously counterintuitive outcomes within the politico-economic landscape.

> If there has been discussion about the reasons for and the effects of privatizing social services which, at least in some capitalist states, had been considered the obligation of the state, reference to the privatization of prisons and of military services is rare. But what are

we to do in theoretical terms about the fact that military services are increasingly organized in the form of private business (2011, p. 77)?

This jarring reality places the US state in an unaccustomed light: a state that still directs public revenues, maintains regulatory structure, but services its needs in cooperation with corporate agents. It not only facilitates capital, but also mobilizes public spending for the good of capital, not as a 'bailout' but as a structural characteristic of public spending. This harnessing of corporations as public agents sits at the center of adaptive accumulation, rendering a symbiotic relationship between state policy objectives and enhanced private revenue streams. Ultimately, it captures a concrete manifestation of the dynamics highlighted within critical institutionalism: the moment in which social agents seek to utilise and/or change the terms of an institutional form, rather than have their action delimited by it.

The concept of adaptive accumulation also exhibits a close affinity with well-known arguments in political economy concerning neoliberalism, insofar as it points to the social validation of market 'efficiencies' and the denouncement of public spending 'wastage'. Probably the most frequently cited work in this regard is David Harvey's notion of accumulation-by-dispossession. Harvey (2005) argues that Marx's concept of primitive accumulation, wherein social relations, property possession and power are radically altered, need not be confined historically to the original transition to capitalism. Rather, he describes (largely by way of numerous examples) an ongoing and constitutive part of neoliberal capitalism as just that: the appropriation of old and new terrains upon which to proceed with accumulation (2005, pp. 145–167). This can happen *via* force as surely as it can occur through re-regulation, but the end goal is always to enhance possibilities for private profits. The concept has certainly taken its fair share of criticism, most notably for its unusually wide breadth, incorporating such a large array of normal capitalist processes that its analytical purchase is left open to question (Brenner, 2006). But it is worth noting that accumulation-by-dispossession reawakened in political economic research the integral importance of state power in 'aiding and abetting' increased capital accumulation across a variety of circumstances. Rather than viewing neoliberalism through the lens of ideological fervor on the part of the state, Harvey redirected our attention to its complicity in a form of thievery or hijacking of non-capitalistic mechanisms for instrumentalist, private objectives.

For all that is made of its theoretical broadness, accumulation-by-dispossession still resonates in the current era, as privatization remains the default solution to almost any societal/organizational issue. As Harvey (2005) put it, the "... reversion of common property rights won through years of hard class struggle (the right to a state pension, to welfare, to national healthcare) to the private do- main has been one of the most egregious of all policies of dispossession pursued in the name of neoliberal orthodoxy" (2005, p. 148). My own writing on biomed- ical research and healthcare underlines this reality, pointing to a concerted push to open up old (universal health) and new (intellectual property, trade in serv- ices) arenas for private profit streams (Loeppky, 2010, 2014). But that research also points to the shortfalls of dispossession, stressing the deliberate calcula- tions of capital, particularly in its delicate entry into spheres of public interest. Indeed, Harvey's version of neoliberal practices positions the state and its citi- zenry as subjects of considerable gullibility, while the *fait accompli* of 'grand theft public' leaves their most prized and hard-earned possessions expropriated by private actors. Importantly, however, the fate of the US public domain has been more deliberately transformed, by state and corporate actors alike, in ways that not only preserve its status and size, but also utilize its potential.

In this way, adaptive accumulation distances us from a singular image of ne- oliberal change, associated with the archetype of lean regulation, state sell-offs, and a general retrenchment from the public arena. The structures of public insti- tutions can and do provide invaluable platforms from which to enter or expand new avenues of private accumulation. Public objectives can be harnessed, such that a stable stream of revenue flows for private actors undertaking public tasks, ostensibly with a new integrity or effectiveness. The goal is not to remove the spec- ter of government involvement or organization, but rather to subject its operational- ization to private actors. In this sense, adaptive accumulation often involves advoca- cy for stronger government involvement, not less. None of this follows a predetermined path, and its outcomes are the subject of struggle between corpo- rate agents, component parts of the state, and popular movements. Advanta- geous policy structures are both fought for and defended, as they are "... treated as products of action through time ... a pattern of social relations, which can be competitive, oppositional and characterised by unequal power relations" (Jenson and Mérand, 2010, p. 82). Adaptive accumulation highlights the attention paid by corporate agents to read signals not only of the market but of legislative and regulatory fields. The total effect of this—in health, military, education, pris- ons—presents an image of American capitalism that, rather than being lean and anti-interventionist, contains a strong dose of state largesse and corporate de- pendence.

In the highly competitive environment that neoliberalism has spawned, adaptive accumulation serves participant actors on a number of fronts. The *first* of these is primary for any accumulative dynamic: profit. The opportunity for profit stands at the center of all capitalist endeavors, but here profit can be generated in a more stable and structured manner. Capital is able to utilize the stability of government functions, adapting them to the degree that is politically and momentarily feasible, in order to channel new or enhanced private returns. And this, "need not always imply the erosion or dissolution of institutional formulations ... [but] can very well mean the maintenance or even expansion of these formations," all in an effort by a given industrial sector "... to firewall itself from the debilitating effects of market competition" (Loeppky, 2010, p. 62). In other words, with government monopsonies, comes a higher level of predictability—guaranteed contracts, political lobbying and favoritism, and the promise of expansion.

Governmental actors, too, find promise in this relationship, during an era in which budgetary reach has been greatly curtailed. While it is consistently true that government involvement in most areas has been under ideological siege for some time, the social expectations placed on the state to 'deliver' does not appear to have waned. In an ongoing era of austerity, when budgetary leanness is the order of the day, public authorities at all levels struggle to deliver something—anything—to their constituents. This has been true in the US particularly since the 1990s, as Congress sought to undue the spending trends of the previous administration (while blaming Democrats). Cuts to Medicaid, welfare assistance, and state block grants did, indeed, balance the federal budget. But rather than signaling a new opportunity for social investment, budget success ushered in an onslaught of tax reductions in the 2000s, thinning out the revenue base of both federal and state governments, just as the Bush Administration mounted two major military campaigns. In the post-2008 environment, the Obama Administration made little headway in reversing this situation, with the revenue base only modestly increased, at the cost of a gargantuan political struggle with Republicans in Congress. Meanwhile, state and municipal budgets continue to labour under constant strain, and the appetite for revenue boosting (raising taxes) at the lower levels of government is paltry.

This is why the routinization of budgets through capped contracts is attractive to policymakers. When such fixed arrangements are tendered out to the most competitive (or well connected) bidder, it meets the criteria of austerity while ensuring an ongoing and central role for policymakers in the distribution and utilization of public revenues. This is perfectly in line with those who have made the assertion that neither neoliberalism nor globalization have occasioned the dissolution or even retrenchment of the state (Panitch, 1994). On the contrary, re-regulation along neoliberal lines requires no less of a state apparatus, simply one that is more highly attuned to the needs of capital. Within this milieu, adaptive accumulation allows state agents to take political credit for managerial intervention in public affairs; satisfies a politico-cultural thirst for 'market-based solutions'; and affords them the luxury of distance from the day-to-day opera-tions of public utility (with exceptions only in moments of scandal or crisis).

This leads to a *second* function of adaptive accumulation, whereby corpora-tions exhibit a more productive—rather than merely hostile—relationship to pub-lic institutions. In many areas of public policy, like prisons and education, there is an assumption that policy goals will be pursued with a public, non-commodi-fied purpose. A public mandate requires, in other words, that its execution will not be for the purposes of profit accumulation, and privatization could only be justified in the wake of evidence-based arguments (Jing, 2010). Unfortunately, such rigorous scrutiny rarely holds and, instead, core governmental functions are ceded to private actors through the construction of 'crisis'. 'Crisis' is the ave-nue by which reform agendas are promulgated and pursued, as public functions under the weight of thinning revenues are positioned as under-performing, inef-ficient, and on the edge of collapse. In these ostensible moments of peril, there is a less-than-subtle neoliberal critique of state administrative capacity. Paradoxi-cally, however, there is also the recognition that whatever public function is being pursued, it has inherent value for society. Otherwise, why would its disso-lution constitute a crisis?

It is this undercurrent of public value that offers both policymaker and cap-ital alike the opportunity to enter into 'accountability' displays, making an exhi-bition of public-private contracts through which services can be deployed in pre-sumably more responsible ways. Labeling this uniquely as dispossession *via* privatization (as in Harvey) bypasses an important point: there needs to be a continuing presence of public utility—actual or otherwise—in order to legitimize both the generation of public revenues and envelop participant corporations in public responsibility. Policymakers are then said not to be opening the door for private accumulation, but rather finding the most efficacious pathway to rescu-ing public objectives, with both equity and quality in mind. Corporate bodies are not just seeking new pathways to profit, but rather fulfilling valuable societal functions. The objective is not simply to shore up 'failed' government functions, but rather to carry them out in a transformed manner, such that the conversion of public revenues into private accumulation is, in the first instance, the execu-tion of legitimate public policy. This quasi-public status for private actors is why remaining governmental function cannot disappear altogether in these sectors—they provide both the signal of hope for society's betterment (mostly through ap-propriations) and the crisis-ridden (and resource-starved) institution for which the private sector positions itself as the new public saviour.

Finally, we would be remiss to gloss over the fact that, in spite of available evidence, adaptive accumulation seems to retain public appeal. There is no shortage of defenders when it comes to market players' involvement in governmental function. In this way, once private actors are an integral part of policy, a *third* function of adaptive accumulation emerges: to stoke a broad public sentiment along reactionary lines. From the late 1970s, it remains true that considerable (or at least enough) public support for increasingly right-wing public policy has furnished a political basis from which restructuring could proceed. And therein lies the surprise: neoliberal arguments of 'reform' have proven highly attractive to medium- to low-income populations, squarely running counter to their actual material interests. The siphoning off of public revenues, growing inequality, accelerated achievement gaps, and irrationally aggressive law-and-order practices all meet with relative acquiescence on the center-left and enthusiasm on the right. The active presence of corporate agents in policy—as patriotic guardians of public purpose—upends the association of social justice to governmental work. And to the extent that adaptive accumulation gains a stronger foothold in areas of social delivery, the deeper seems to be the societal recoil when these public-private arrangements are criticized.

Critics of neoliberalism—and especially current manifestations of right-wing neoliberalism in the US—have typically positioned populist support as a form revanchist politics. In moments of crisis, class anxiety can lead to a dangerous form of authoritarian appeal, particularly in its intent to accord blame (Langman, 2012). As such, one usually finds a quest to recover a morally superior past, as well as a 'status anxiety' that derives from a sense of loss. This loss, linked to an over-mythologized existence of the productive protestant work ethic, is then connected to state intervention that is seen to be shoring up 'parasitic' classes (the poor, minorities, immigrants, etc.). This gives rise to resentment that can be channeled at identifiable demographics—perhaps the oppressive Northeastern liberal, black communities or unions. Bundled into the broad category of the 'undeserving' and those who advocate on their behalf, these groups become legitimate targets that are said to have sidestepped personal blame (and responsibility) within a puritan, individualistic ethic. Martin Konings (2012) has emphasized that this politics is anxiety driven, giving rise to a paradoxical back-and-forth between resentment and redemption, through the adoption of hyper-neoliberal values that, effectively, scorn a caricatured 'other'. These values, in turn, feed a needed sense of political agency, where a puritan brand of neoliberal ideology offers the opportunity to discipline, leading to a personal purification and a hoped-for redemptive return to an imagined republican polity.

Adaptive accumulation, then, contributes to an ethos in which not only corporate agency is sanctified, but state involvement is vilified and treated with scorn. Local communities continue to advocate for the expansion of private prisons in their districts, and the charter school movement has never been so popular. Over the past few decades, little has blocked the dynamic growth in these public policy arenas, and each has primed itself for expansion on a yearly basis. There are moments in which public criticism seems to catch fire in political circles, but just as quickly, it is spirited away. The interventions of Black Lives Matter, in the wake of media attention to police aggression and mass community protest, has had an impact on public discussions of racialized incarceration rates. Isolated moments of criticism for education companies have highlighted the questionable basis upon which for-profit schools proceed. Perhaps most tellingly, the eruption and then demonization of the Medicare for All proposal signals a deep seeded mistrust of the health industry but also, paradoxically, governmental interruption of existing private healthcare. Simply put, there exists no broad and sustained popular movement calling into question the operation of private capital in profitable but often questionable relationships with core public programs. And the mainstream of the Democratic party, along with the sharpened edge of a now transformed Republican party, appear largely unequipped to challenge this scenario.

Taken together, these three functional attributes foster the attractiveness of adaptive accumulation within given policy areas, for both governmental and corporate actors. But they also point to limitations in the conventional manner in which US political economy is depicted. The portrayal of a lean, minimalist state, with a free market of hyper-competitive actors, does not really capture the circumstances of a very considerable portion of contemporary US neoliberal practice. The problem with folding these circumstances into the mould of Anglo-American neoliberalism is that it blinds us to the fact that such outcomes, "do not emanate from the existence of some abstract and purified entity named the market, but result from struggles over the institutions and regulations, which define markets as concrete sites for economic activity" (Knafo and Teschke, 2020, p. 90). Put another way, unbridled neoliberalism, quite simply, is seen to unleash a torrent of private contracts, and this forms the basis upon which the U.S. is compared to its peer countries, which are seen to have a greater (and more successful) politico-cultural and institutional inclination towards governmental intervention. However, as the cases below make clear, neither market advocates in US governmental circles nor corporate actors are uniformly against governmental intervention. On the contrary, governmental and corporate agents have adapted their position on state involvement, innovating its form rather than rejecting it outright. This innovative agency needs to be taken seriously, as it has evolved to make up a very large—and problematic—component of US wealth accumulation. Such approaches to neoliberal accumulation are counter-intuitive, because "knowing what is new about an innovation when it emerges is something difficult to grasp. It cannot be read off directly from the [politico-economic] context in which it occurs" (2020, p. 94). As such, the remainder of this work is devoted to elucidating empirical cases of adaptive accumulation, with an eye to understanding neoliberalism in terms that emanate from its actual historical reality, rather than our rather stylized images of US capitalism.

Chapter 3: The Military and Adaptive Accumulation

The most extensive relationship that the US government has with private actors is quite regularly—and rather casually—referred to as the 'military-industrial complex' (MIC). This concept is meant to summarize a web of connections between Congressional payers, decision-making bureaucrats and industrial producers, with officials moving between industry and government to bring about oligopolistic profits through the weapons procurement process. Undoubtedly, the productive outcome of this industrial complex reaches staggering proportions: in 2015, while worldwide arms sales reached $370 billion, companies based in the U.S. accounted for over $200 billion of those sales (SIPRI, 2016). This is, in part, brought about by a political culture deeply imbued with themes of militarism, national security, and threat discourse, and the bipartisan spending largesse of Congress on the Department of Defense (DOD) reflects the potency of this political culture. And the unwieldy nature of weapons spending has been the subject of popular and academic analysis since Dwight D. Eisenhower's famous reference to the MIC in his presidential farewell address (Fallows, 2002).

This chapter, however, is not about weapons procurement, because it is not an adaptive strategy, either on the part of business or the US government. While it can be understood to have a public purpose, weapons production has always involved the intertwined activities of corporations and government, with the latter explicitly relying on the former. Even before Eisenhower's warning, there never existed any meaningful, non-corporate alternative, and private producers, while jockeying with one another to some degree, have never really had to adapt their accumulation strategies, *per se*. More importantly, the regular process of procurement contracts involves the production and then *handover* of military hardware, albeit at bloated and politically-laden prices. There is no ensuing public or quasi-public role for corporate actors in the wake of hardware production.

Stepping outside the purchase and sale of weaponry, it is instructive to consider the nature of government expenditures across the entire US defense budget, which reached $700 billion in 2018. Across this wider fiscal context, the prevalence of adaptive accumulation becomes more readily apparent. This chapter explores the manner and extent to which DOD's responsibilities as a public institution have more recently been handed off to private contractors, in the name cost-saving, efficiency and long-term strategic viability. At the same time, it considers the manner in which corporate actors have recognized and acted on the opportunity to make the military a leaner institution. As it turns out, the imperatives of both an austerity-driven budget environment and the strategic demands

https://doi.org/10.1515/9783110761801-003

of a post-Cold War military apparatus generate profitable and long-term spheres of private activity.

To do this, the chapter begins with a discussion of the military as an arena of public policy. It does so to dissolve the artificial line—regularly utilized in US budgetary discussions—between military and non-military spending. Foreign policy is still public policy, albeit with an outward, geopolitical perspective, and it serves public purpose. The chapter emphasizes the changing budgetary demands that have emerged since the Cold War, with an eye to understanding transformations in the public nature of the military's activities. It then proceeds to explore the altered conditions of military engagement, which involve private contracting in an extensive and expanding manner. Along the way, the crux of debate around such contracting has focused on precisely the issues germane to public policy: citizens'/soldiers' well-being, efficacy, and accountability. Each of these has been indelibly altered while the potential for accumulation among private contractors has grown. Finally, the chapter turns to the domestic front, examining the changing conditions of US bases, where military policy reaches more deeply into the daily lives of US citizens, and where private contractors have entered the scene in a problematic manner. The total picture painted is one of military policy that feigns public objectives but that channels enormous social wealth into corporate actors' revenue streams, with the latter rarely held to any measure of meaningful public accountability.

3.1 Defense Policy as Public Policy

In discussions of public policy, national security and defense matters are often—if not always—handled in a compartmentalized fashion, ostensibly sheltered from the political nature of domestic matters. On its face, defense is expected to be both bipartisan and, to a large extent, apolitical. Paradoxically, this bipartisanship is enforced through the almost guaranteed political firestorm that results from criticizing the military, an act mostly perceived as undercutting the well-being of US service personnel. In a political culture where military honour and the sanctity of the citizen-soldier are revered, dispassionate assessments of defense-related budgets and policy are the subject of political caution. Anything else invites charges of being 'soft on defense' or 'against the troops', which is obviously unpalatable for any political actor.

This compartmentalization is as intellectual as it is political. Witness the division across academe between the study of political science/public policy and that of security and defense programs. In the past, "the public policy field largely ceded questions of traditional defense and national security policy to international relations and security scholars" (Archuleta, 2016, p. S51). Much of this division emerged during the Cold War and onward, but the autonomous 'security intellectual' is still largely sectioned off from the confines of either political science or public policy departments. Indeed, the emergence of 'strategic studies' programs, which morphed into security studies after the end of the Cold War, has always suggested that the logic applicable to defense/military matters is separate from the study of politics or policy more generally. Whether it is in the logic of deterrence, structural realism, geopolitics, or any other form of security discourse, socio-political understandings of military policy or the policy process remain, for the most part, sidelined. In a survey study of public policy research, Brandon Archuleta (2016) has suggested that, "policy scholars should note that there were practically no published articles relating to the Department of the Defense—the nation's largest bureaucracy—during the 2011 to 2015 window. This is both revealing and disturbing" (2016, p. S56).

On a political level, this artificial division is made evident in the ongoing budget process of sequestration, an instrument put in place during the Congressional budgetary crisis of 2011. Under sequestration, a failure to find bipartisan consensus on a long-term budget instigates automatic cuts across government departments, equally impacting military and non-military spending. This arrangement is designed to hurt each political party in the area they prioritize, should they fail to make adequate political compromises. It is, of course, highly debatable whether Democrats meaningfully 'deprioritize' defense spending, particularly when spending is contracted and sub-contracted in ways that affect virtually every congressional district (Thorpe, 2010). More significantly for this discussion, however, sequestration also preserves military policy as an autonomous sphere, defensible on non-budgetary grounds, such as national security, patriotism, and military honour. Quite simply, how budgetary resources are apportioned and utilized (the policy process) are subject to less scrutiny when held up against these larger political and dramatic narratives.

In plain terms, however, defense policy *is* public policy, and the process by which government revenues are distributed for either service or product should be understood no differently than any other department. Currently, this is not the case, as public revenues are viewed differently when appropriated for military purpose. Whatever one's moral or political disposition towards military activities, the fact remains that such activities bring no direct 'returns on investment'. They are public activities, orchestrated by public institutions and employees, and they have distinctly public, non-monetary objectives, at least in an immediate sense. As such, they should be subject to the same assessment as other public activities. Do they meet their stated objective? Who benefits from this public policy? How has this policy changed over time, and have such changes affected the nature of its outcomes? Such assessments do reveal considerable alterations over time, particularly since the Reagan administration, which ushered in a contradictory blend of increased budgetary largesse and a stepped up approach to austerity.

3.2 Peace Dividends: Do More with Less (or More?)

In retrospect, the 1980s amounted to a monumental and transformational period in American military policy. The decade was bookended by two revolutionary changes: the Reagan Revolution at the outset and the end of the Cold War as the decade drew to a close. In the first, the Reagan administration manifested a wider politico-ideological turn towards increasingly austerity-oriented government, complemented (often in a contradictory fashion) by spikes in defense spending. The philosophy of neoliberal governance has been well told elsewhere, but it generally involved less government service; more individual responsibility; a redistributed (increasingly regressive) taxation base and, above all, privatization (Harvey, 2011). The ideological lock hold that privatization has held across particularly Anglo-American governments and societies has manifested as a policy 'cure-all' to the quandaries of governance, wherein the efficiencies of the marketplace are understood to correct the inefficiencies of bureaucratic inertia. There is no reason that military decision makers should be immune to this rhetoric, as "governments succumbed to an ideological trend towards privatization of many of their functions: a whole raft of former state responsibilities—including education, policing, and the operation of prisons—were turned over to the marketplace" (Singer, 2005, p. 120). While many of these areas will be considered in the chapters that follow, it is sufficient for the purposes of this chapter that a general environment of market-friendly governmental techniques has increasingly been the norm since the Reagan Administration.

The second stream of developments, the end of the Cold War and the collapse of East European political regimes, ushered in an era of so-called peace dividends. Without the ongoing perception of threat emanating from the Warsaw Pact, political justification for the large-scale projection of US military presence became increasingly untenable. Up through the Clinton Administration and into the first Bush Administration, defense spending was constrained, which gave rise to an extensive rethink on the military positioning of the United States. This was as much an academic as a practical exercise, conceptualizing what the role of the military would be moving forward, and what constituted the central 'threats' of the 21st century (Tuchman Mathews, 1989; Sorensen, 1990). And as the 1990s proceeded, the array of potential 'threats' for the US military seemed to be growing rather than becoming more limited—terrorism, biological warfare, humanitarian intervention, environmental security, drug wars, and the list went on. As the costs of hardware outpaced inflation, and as the potentiality of restricted budgets became a growing reality (particularly in the Clinton Administration), the Department of Defense (DOD) was encouraged to do more with less, a lesson it no doubt acted upon.

Through this transitional conceptual and budgetary period, there emerged a renewed interest in both the so-called revolution in military affairs (RMA) and the total force concept. In the former, the military re-evaluated its position in relation to prevailing threats in the global environment. This re-evaluation suggested the need for war fighting capacity that did not focus on one massive campaign, but instead the ability to project force on multiple fronts. Much of this hinged on the progression of technologies—aerospace, missile technology, drones, satellites, etc.—to ensure that the brunt of conflict could be orchestrated remotely (Freedman, 1998; O'Hanlon, 1998). It also meant the aggressive development and procurement of advanced military hardware, particularly those related to air power and precision weaponry. Armed with enhanced technology, America could conceivably fight emergent threats in locales where the conventional insertion of its fighting force would present costly challenges. The maintenance of advanced hardware on this level is increasingly expensive to maintain. As such, budgetary pressure in this arena, with the exception of brief restraint during the Clinton Administration, has never really subsided and, arguably, has intensified.

Simultaneously, the post-Cold War world's peace prospects brought calls for a reduced fighting force, as the central threat of Soviet (and then Russian) power projection receded. The necessity of standing professional personnel was diminished, with a fall back to continental defense and more limited engagement abroad. With this, the notion of total force utilization was revitalized, mostly focused on the total combined utilization of professional personnel, reserve forces and national guard units. This was not in itself a transformation; the total force concept had been in play for decades before the fall of the Berlin Wall and was debated extensively through the Vietnam War (Correll, 2011). But the implications of such policies were surely foreseeable: with a heavier segment of forces constituted by non-professional personnel (voluntary or involuntary), the political liability of deployment became much greater. When combined with both austerity politics and the ever-increasing procurement demands of DOD, an inevitable series of changes to personnel would emerge, with an eye to reducing this political liability.

It is worth restating here that the objective of adaptive accumulation is not merely to shore up perceived public failings; it is to transform public functions into politically legitimated private revenue streams. Both public figures and private actors envision the opportune moment to create new arenas of investment growth and durable government contracting. And, as with all things DOD, this would not be on a small scale. Armed forces, especially those deployed, require a great deal of logistic, technical and supportive infrastructure. And, conventionally, the military—as a public institution—has rounded out this infrastructure with a personnel force that is widely varying in its skillset and largely self-sufficient in its capacities. Doctors, cooks, clerks, engineers, and an endless list of infrastructural support personnel have made this self-sufficiency possible.

Since all personnel—militarily engaged or otherwise—remain both a large budgetary component and politically sensitive in periods of deployment, the possibility that non-public, market actors could 'voluntarily' fill some of these positions has been presented as an attractive prospect. It is certainly the case that large infrastructural sections of the military labor force require no formal military or combat training and are, thus, serviceable by outside contract. Contracting, in turn, appears to further a two-fold objective. In budgetary terms, set contracts with private corporations suggest sound fiscal management, with fixed global payouts and seemingly more effective market-inspired (not bureaucratic) management. In political terms, then, the public image of deployment can be focused on only professional forces, appearing to reduce the number of US military personnel in harm's way. All of this has led to a pattern of US military spending over the last two decades which has dramatically widened and accelerated the transfer of public funds to private actors.

3.3 Transforming Power Projection Abroad

What was once a minor phenomenon within US force projection is now a major element of its military deployments. Wherever one falls on the desirability of an enlarged defense budget (e. g. so-called hawks vs. doves), the introduction of private provision in war-fighting capabilities raises immediate and large-scale concerns, not the least of which is public accountability. In general, DOD has a contracted workforce which amounts to about 33 percent of its active duty force, a number estimated at 710,000 in 2011 (US Government Accountability Office, 2013, p. 8). As a general trend, these numbers are certainly high, but they are demonstrably more alarming when considered in the context of deployment. While from WWII to the First Persian Gulf War, contracting amounted to 5–10 percent of personnel deployment, subsequent US campaigns relied much more heavily on such arrangements. In the Balkans, Afghanistan and Iraq, private contracting as a component of total US deployment exceeded 50 percent (Schwartz and Swain, 2011, p. 2). This contracting represents a staggering alteration in the manner in which DOD has utilized public revenues during contingency operations.

DOD has moved swiftly since the First Gulf War to ramp up its contingency operations *via* market contracting, ensuring that US military adventurism is both politically less sensitive and, along the way, a lucrative profit sphere. The most controversial element of this projection has undoubtedly been the utilization of private military forces (PMF), in order to bolster US operations in a manner that simultaneously reduces the exposure of US military personnel. PMFs are corporate organizations that fill a variety of roles in relation to force projection, from military advising to logistical support. According to Peter Singer (2005),

> [the] industry is divided into three basic sectors: military provider firms (also known as "private security firms"), which offer tactical military services, including actual combat services, to clients; military consulting services, which employ retired officers to provide strategic advice and military training; and military support firms, which provide logistics, intelligence and maintenance services to armed forces, allowing the latter's soldiers to concentrate on combat and reducing their government's need to recruit more troops or call up more reserves (2005, p. 120).

DOD utilizes a very extensive workforce that is based on private security firms of one sort or another. By 2010, there were over 260,000 personnel contracted in the field by DOD, State and USAID, but over 200,000 of these were contracted by Defense. The fact that this figure, which varies over time, often exceeds the numbers that are publicly employed suggests a remarkable reliance on non-defense personnel (Commission on Wartime Contracting in Iraq and Afghanistan, 2011, p. 20).

Certainly, the most acute cases of controversy in relation to PMFs are those instances in which the potential for combat or violent activity exists. This involves personnel who work in convoy escort, personal security or general base security, who are subject to extensive risk. The utilization of such forces can be surprisingly large, rising to over 15,000 in Afghanistan by 2011. As missions became subject to the 'light footprint' approach of the Obama Administration, so too did the less-than visible use of contracting in both Afghanistan and Iraq, where, respectively, a contractor-to-military ratio of 3:1 and 2:1 became the norm (Zenko, 2016). One major difficulty with the utilization of such forces is that they are not subject to the same rules of engagement as a publicly employed soldier. There is an unregulated ethos that surrounds their deployment, and their training, activities and methods largely go unverified. As such, any potential or real engagement in combat situations is not subject to the same process of public accountability, either in terms of its effect on the surrounding population or in the safety and well-being of these same personnel. Ultimately, there is no way to quantify the overall impact of PMF forces, but the fact that not one PMF contractor has been held to account in Iraq, even following Abu Ghraib and various Blackwater scandals, speaks volumes (Singer, 2005, pp. 127–128).

At the same time, the stark reality of contractor deaths is also quite telling. Between 2001 and 2011, there were 6,131 deaths among US military personnel, but there were also 2,429 deaths among privately contracted forces (Commission on Wartime Contracting in Iraq and Afghanistan, 2011, p. 31). Given that the total number of US combat forces throughout that time period was enormous, the casualty ratio for privately contracted forces (involved in combat) were astronomically higher. And this higher ratio was brought into dramatic relief under the Obama administration, during which more private contractors died than US military personnel. Even with such casualty ratios, there is no public outcry over the loss of these personnel; indeed, there is little public reflection on the matter at all. The difference with deaths in relation to PMFs is the weak responsibility demonstrated by corporations on reporting, along with their detachment from public policy and accountability.

Incidences of combat or violence outside the military chain of command did not evolve haphazardly or by accident. Both political figures and corporate actors prefer this arrangement:

> Giving birth to such markets is just one of the many ways that contractors encourage dangerous policymaking. Unlike the Pentagon or CIA, private military companies do not report to Congress, circumventing democratic accountability of the armed forces. Worse, they shield themselves from inquiry by invoking the need to protect proprietary information and are not subject to Freedom of Information Act requests, unlike the military or intelligence community. This makes them ideal for dangerous missions requiring plausible deniability. Sometimes, even Congress can't find out what these firms do (McFate, 2016).

Cloaked in proprietary secrecy, the utilization of these forces in combat situations has been carefully nurtured across corporate and political lines. There has been a deliberate re-drawing of the boundaries that nominally demarcate 'mercenary' from legitimate combat behaviours. In this regard, PMF actions are carefully portrayed as 'self-defense' by their supporters, legitimizing their activities in the face of the 'anti-mercenary' norm (Petersohn, 2014). This re-characterization has been underway in Congressional circles since the Bush administration, whereby testimony given on behalf of PMFs, buttressed by select political figures, has strenuously insisted that private forces are tasked with security and threat avoidance, not progressive combat (2014, p. 489).

The discursive shift to 'self-defense' in the face of unambiguous combat involvement allows for a powerful representational tool in relation to all PMF activities. Corporations, from DynaCorp to Halliburton, are ostensibly not pursuing profit, but instead protecting American well-being. The association of sacrifice for public purpose (defending US troops and advancing US interests), while insisting that they are not 'guns for hire', creates a virtuous rhetorical scenario. The Obama administration could remain below or at the Congressional limit on deployed US military in Iraq and Afghanistan, precisely because it could pay for under-the-radar services of PMFs. Meanwhile, the private nature of such undertakings could be registered politically as civic duty rather than profit accumulation—this, despite the fact that a majority of combat-ready personnel hired on contract are foreign nationals, presumably uninterested in US civic well-being or the public purpose inherent in US national interests.

The combat component of PMF contracts, however, comprises a smaller percentage of their activities. In fact, privately-contracted infrastructural support constitutes the mainstay of PMF revenues, and also the most lucrative. In line with the abovementioned budgetary imperatives, military bases that can be constructed and maintained by private civilian forces eliminate DOD-orchestrated tasks, ostensibly with an eye to costs savings. However, if such fixed contracts hold the potential for cost savings, they are not immediately obvious to the casual observer, as DOD outlays for base support grew astronomically since the outset of the Afghanistan War. Such outlays, of course, translate into an expansive growth of business proceeds for eligible corporations. All told, between 2001 and 2013, DOD's estimated spending on such contracts totals $385 billion dollars (Vine, 2014, p. 83). It is important to keep in mind that these tasks were once publicly arranged and internally executed by the US military, now transformed into private revenue streams and base service delivery.

Whether such transformations signal anything akin to efficiency is certainly open to question. The Commission on Wartime Contracting (CWC) issued a "sobering but conservative estimate" of $31–60 billion in contract waste and fraud in US operations in Afghanistan and Iraq (Commission on Wartime Contracting in Iraq and Afghanistan, 2011, p. 1). The CWC highlights the tentative nature of this number, and commentators have insisted that efficacy of these contracts is impossible to determine, as DOD monitoring and enforcement of contractual obligations remains weak. While the vast majority of bases in Afghanistan and Iraq have now been closed, there are still over 800 non-domestic bases that utilize private contracting in both build and maintenance operations. Taken together, two-thirds of public funds used in contracts in both contingency operations and global base deployment have involved private services, ranging from 'logistics' to professional services to building maintenance. This ongoing base projection involves a clear concentration of public largesse, wherein a definitive set of corporate actors benefits the most (though they are hardly alone). In Iraq and Afghanistan, between 2002 and 2011, for instance, 22 firms benefited to the tune $192.5 billion, or 52 percent of all contracts (2011, p. 25).

The redirected funding of bases has changed the nature of deployment while making base maintenance an arena of profiteering, reasonably removed from the critical eye of domestic oversight. The basic debate around private contracting, of course, remains the same,

> ... driven in part by unresolved questions about relative costs between the two sectors. Some argue that government is inherently less expensive because it does not need to make a profit. Others argue that government is generally more expensive because it does not need to compete and to be efficient to remain in business. Where commentators come down depends strongly on their views about government and the private sector, with Republicans generally relying more on the private sector and Democrats more on government (Cancian, 2019, p. 11).

David Vine (2014) has documented this utilization of public revenues, though he and others have been forthright about the difficulty of tracking DOD spending. He has made clear that even following the relative drawdown in Iraq and Afghanistan, his conservative estimates on foreign base spending is in the range of $150 billion per year (Vine, 2017). The point is repeatedly made by commentators that such extensive budgetary redirection into the private sectors does not bring about savings:

> With respect to the market in private military services ... there is reason to believe that outsourcing increases the cost of military functions. There are two major reasons for this. First, a transparent and competitive market is necessary if clients are to pick and choose among different suppliers. Second, for a market to be efficient, contracts must be subject to transparent bidding procedures; competing offers must be systematically compared; and the performance of suppliers on the contract terms has to be closely monitored—and, if necessary, sanctioned. None of these characteristics seems to apply to current contracting procedures, however. In truth, the market for private security services is only partially competitive, and in some cases—in certain areas of logistics, for example—quasi-monopolistic. The defenders of the virtues of privatization and outsourcing with respect to the military generally forget one thing: The Pentagon is as far removed from a free market as one can possibly get (Isenberg, 2011, para.7).

Indeed, as far as savings go, Vine (2014) makes clear that contractors probably saddle the US government with costs at a level twice or triple what it would pay were a public official to undertake the same task (2014, p. 94). In this revenue environment, base and infrastructural contractors seek to add 'ice cream' to facilities, referring to indulgences provided to troops, ostensibly making their tour more agreeable (2014, p. 95). To fulfill such heightened expectations, an array of private actors, including dominant players like Kellog, Brown & Root (KBR), Supreme Group, Agility Logistics, DynCorp and BP, have sought repeated access to a large number of contracts in Iraq, Afghanistan and well beyond. The aim here is not to procure savings in public dollars, but to capitalize on budgetary largesse aimed at an enhanced 'military experience'.

The outcome of these arrangements cannot be overemphasized: normalization of and dependence on private sector personnel as means to US military projection. Whether in relation to contingency operations or more permanent forward deployment scenarios, the greater the reliance of the US military on private contracting for administrative, logistical or low-order security tasks, the weaker the public institutional capacity available to carry out such tasks. As Anne Leander (2005) has pointed out,

> Supply in the market for force is self-perpetuating. It creates its own demand. As PMCs become security experts, lobbyists and consultants, they shape security understandings of clients who consequently require increasing levels of service. The clients whose demand the market responds to include both those contesting and those defending security orders. The consequence is a strain on ... public security orders. The strain is accentuated because the market for force drains resources from public security establishments and undermines their legitimacy, hence making contestation both from the inside and the outside more likely (2005, p. 618).

Whatever one's moral and political disposition towards such deployment, this carving out of present and future contracting domains is precisely what underwrites adaptive accumulation. It does not exactly mimic the heavily monopolized dynamic of the weapons procurement complex. After all, as Vine (2014) rightly points out, between 2001 and 2013, an astounding 1.7 million separate contracts were tendered, with an enormous variation of tasks (2014, p. 88). This suggests an extensive *marketplace* of contract activity, wherein a competitive dynamic is certainly 'massaged' by dominant firms and their political connections, but it is hardly eliminated. At the same time, there is no corporate desire to replace public revenues and governmental power through the direct private acquisition of military force (for instance, with corporate actors purchasing such military capabilities outside the parameters of the US government). Instead, private actors encourage the circumstances in which Pentagon spending in the base world has been marked by spiraling expenditures, the growing use of contracts lacking incentives to control costs, sometimes criminal behavior, and the repeated awarding of non-competitive sweetheart contracts to companies with histories of fraud and abuse (2014, p. 91). All of this can be perpetuated under a guise of patriotic citizenship, whereby PMFs ostensibly perform a public service in which they place country before corporation.

3.4 On the Homefront: Utilities and Housing

It is not only the forward deployment of US military forces that affords unique accumulation opportunities. As part of the 1990s 'peace dividend', domestic military installations were also subject to roving cost control. This has certainly been manifested in long-term base realignment and closure (BRAC), an ongoing and politically touchy consolidation process of installations, assets and personnel across the U.S. (Daniels, 2017; Schnaubelt, 2017). Within this process, there is a reconfiguration of properties across the country, as well as the relocation of tens of thousands of personnel—some 125,000 personnel have been moved as a result of BRAC (US Government Accountability Office, 2010). Base realignment is worthy of mention here, because it is intertwined with the search for 'efficiencies' across all branches of the military, as budgetary control looms over the ever-spiraling nature of defense appropriations. In the aftermath of the Budget Control Act of 2010, sequestration has meant that DOD has been encouraged to find savings, although it has clearly been given more leeway than government social programs. In line with savings sought in forward deployments, war fighting capabilities have been prioritized over support infrastructure. As one analyst insists, it makes "... more sense to fund war fighting activities over construction, [because] facilities degrade more slowly than readiness, and in a constrained budget environment, it is responsible to take risk in facilities first" (Conger, 2018, p. np).

Table 1: Property Managed by US Military, 2016

Military Branch	Buildings	Total Facilities (including structures)	Plant Replacement Value (in billions)	Land (acres)
Army	139,458	278,299	$417.95	13,340,778
Navy	61,368	111,937	$238.50	2,213,663
Air Force	47,738	126,215	$302.58	9,126,467
Marine Corps	26,748	51, 112	$79.40	2,504,943
DOD Total	275,312	568,383	$1,038.43	27,185,851

Source: (US Department of Defense, 2016).

The enormity of base infrastructure cannot be overemphasized. DOD asset holdings, including property and land, are extensive, "with over 500,000 buildings and structures at more than 500 installations, comprising over millions of acres of land spread throughout the United States, U.S. territories and ... 30

other ... countries" (US Department of Defense, n.d.). Table 1 highlights the over-all size of these holdings in 2016, all of which require capital investment, main-tenance, and operational management. In keeping with a budgetary outlook that prioritizes fighting capability over infrastructure, the manner in which such fa-cilities are supported and maintained has been subject to a considerable degree of reform. This has been especially manifested in two areas, utilities and hous-ing, where the Department of Defense has sought to bolster public capacity with private contracts. These areas of contracting are certainly intertwined, as will become evident below, but it is worth handling them discreetly, in order to demonstrate the breadth of adaptive accumulation across domestic military operations.

3.4.1 Utilities

Under the 1990s scramble for cost savings, DOD determined that the US military should not be in the 'business' of utility supply. Utilities refer, in this context, to water, wastewater, electricity and natural gas supply, and the US Congress agreed that these should be supplied by private corporations, subject to qualifi-cations. At the time, in 1997, the military owned some 2600 assets pertaining to utility supply, then valued at $50 billion. Under Public Law 105 – 85, Congress de-termined that utilities not sensitive to national security concerns should be com-petitively tendered to private providers if: "(A) the long-term economic benefit of the [tender] exceeds the long-term economic cost ... and (B) the [tender] will re-duce the long-term costs of the United States for utility services provided by the utility system concerned" (US Congress, 1997, p. 1993). The prevailing assumption was, as usual, that private providers could utilize public revenues more effective-ly, upgrading installations and delivering service at a more economic rate over the long-term. Directing this effort, DOD made definitively clear that all utilities at all bases were to be considered for privatization, and that exceptions should be rare. Indeed, the Deputy Secretary of Defense communicated his expectation that, "Military departments [will] work privatization hard, finding those business innovations that will garner the maximum benefit for the Department and the American taxpayer" (US Deputy Secretary of Defense, 1998). To this effect, it set out a progressive schedule for such transformations, demanding all plans to be submitted by 2000, tenders by 2001, and sale and conveyance contracts in place by 2003.

A full utility selloff and *use of public revenues* to finance the handover to pri-vate providers would not be a popular political position outside of the military. Non-profit providers—whether governmental or semi-autonomous—have a fundamentally different incentive in providing utilities to either consumers or institutional users. The ongoing attempts by private industry to lobby for the sale of the Tennessee Valley Authority and the Bonneville Power Authority have been soundly rejected for this reason on multiple occasions (Conca, 2020). In the same vain, the various branches of the military have proven not-so-enthusiastic on the progressive timetable of utility selloff. And when the Government Accountability Office (GAO) (2005) took stock of this process in the mid-2000s, its findings uncovered considerable justification for this institutional reticence. Outlining the fact that only 94 of 1491 identified facilities had been privatized, its report took serious issue with the overall management of this process. Front and center was the issue of cost, as the GAO (2005) "found that the estimates give an unrealistic sense of savings to a program that generally increases government utility costs in order to pay contractors for enhanced utility services and capital improvements" (2005, p. 4). The report found that in relation to those installations already privatized, involved branches of the military were realizing considerable cost increases. The army estimated a $1.3 million-dollar annual cost increase for every facility privatized. Air Force officials estimated a $100 – 200 million increase over 5 – 10 years of the privatization program (2005, p. 18). Moreover, the report found that tendering and contracts favoured private firms to an unreasonable degree, allowing them to claw back what they paid for the utility through extra-billing. In one demonstrative case, this meant that the Air Force actually paid out 78 percent more than it received for sale (2005, p. 5). And perhaps most ominously, the report also made clear that the monitoring and evaluation of the military was seriously lacking, establishing no independent review for accuracy or compliance over time.

Fast-forward to 2018, and the situation for utility conveyance has not been drastically improved. Another GAO report that attempted to determine cost savings found considerable shortcomings in data and the military's disposition towards contract performance evaluation. Specifically, the report utilized a complete review of 11 different privatization cases, in order to track utility privatization performance and ascertain the degree to which DOD has developed measurable performance standards (US Government Accountability Office, 2018a). It states that "none of the military departments have determined whether the utilities privatization contracts are on track to achieve … cost avoidance estimates" (2018a, p. 14). Besides the same problem with unrealistic initial cost estimates, the examiners found that each contract contains, over time, large numbers of 'modifications', which have a clear effect of increasing cost. At Fort Bragg, for instance, 219 modifications to the contract increased the cost for water and sewage by 96 percent, from $552 million to $1.1 billion over ten years (2018a, p. 15).

In a pattern closely associated with adaptive accumulation, the vast majority of these cost-increasing endeavours are based on 50-year contracts. With some 600 projects now subject to conveyance, private actors find themselves in a sole-source market scenario for their product, and their 'consumer' happens to be the largest purchaser in the world—the US government. Under such a scenario, it seems incumbent on governmental actors to provide evaluation as to whether either quality improvement or cost-saving have been achieved. Stunningly, such evaluations were not discernible to GAO investigators. Instead, the best that was offered to investigators was perception-based, anecdotal evidence. Not only could no long-term data be uncovered regarding either cost saving or service improvement, but there were no meaningful attempts to engage in performance review of utility providers. The military installations in question lacked any settled metrics to assess performance and, as a result, their assessments lacked any basis for what was often a 'satisfactory' review. Of course, the military, like any large bureaucracy, operates on a chain-of-command basis. Here, the GAO could not be clearer: "The military departments have not tracked utilities privatization contract performance and have not developed measurable performance standards because ASD (EI&E)[1] has not issued guidance requiring ... metrics and measurable performance standard" (2018a, p. 18).

As a sure sign that a new arena in which adaptive accumulation has taken hold, industrial players have recently organized a lobby to advance their interests. The creation of Utility Privatization Partners (UPP) is composed of twelve founding member corporations, representing over 100 utility privatization projects (UPP, 2019). While the aim is ostensibly to work with the branches of the military to improve reliability and resilience in utility networks, there is also a direct accumulative objective. The organization has made clear that it "plans to advocate for the evolution and expansion of utilities system partnerships with military installations" (ADC, 2019). On the table, too, will be advocacy for long-term contracts and permissible rate increases, as well as the modeling of performance metrics. The US military pays out more for energy than any institution in the world, 20 percent of which is for electrical and natural gas supply, with water and sewage adding on to this overall utility cost. While the final amount of these utility costs is not extractable from budget figures, they are in the multi-billions per annum. The contracts that tap into this public revenue source, which can also be expanded through infrastructural modifications and upgrades, have become a lucrative, stable, and now quasi-public sphere of accumulation.

---

[1] Assistant Secretary of Defense for Energy, Installations and Environment.

3.4.2 Housing

A year prior to utility privatization, Congress authorized the privatization of military housing, allowing market contracts as a means to build and administer military housing for its personnel on US soil (US Congress, 1996, pp. 2801–2802). At the time, the authorization was intended to foster necessary investment in housing stock—then amounting to some \$20 billion in renovation, build and maintenance costs—that the Pentagon said it could no longer afford. This falls in line with the imperative to preserve available funds for war-fighting capabilities, leaving labour and infrastructure as the chosen domains for cost savings. But it also represents an arena in which there is opportunity to transform ongoing public expenditures into an accrual of private profits.

Proponents characterize the origins and development of military housing privatization as both a herculean and heroic effort. In a history of the US Army's Residential Communities Initiative (RCI), the familiar refrain of slow governmental change being overcome by thoughtful innovators is readily apparent. Accordingly, from its outset, the program is said to have, "faced opposition and doubt from internal and external stakeholders," and that the RCI, "was a new way of doing business and change was not easy for Army leaders and congressional members to accept" (Godfrey *et al.*, 2012, p. 4). The depiction here of government as incapable, slow moving and resistant to change is unmistakable. At the same time, the acknowledgement of what innovation would actually mean— the creation of income streams from public monies—is readily put in the foreground. The aim is to make army housing an attractive business venture, but in a manner that the military itself would fund: "By privatizing housing under the RCI program ... and giving Soldiers the ability to pay rent, the Army created a reliable stream of income that private-sector developers could use for long-term, continuous development" (2012, p. viii). And in a move that clearly puts the imprint of adaptive accumulation on this process, the intentions of developers are projected as extra-commercial in nature. The quasi-public motivations are accentuated, as developers are said to have, "approached their projects as much more than just another business deal," whereby they only entered such arrangements, "because of the true spirit of partnership and patriotism fostered by working for Soldiers and their Families on a daily basis" (2012, pp. xv–xvi). For advocates, the involvement of private actors in military housing has only upsides, and they carefully avoid any underlying problems which may be associated to competitive or profit motives.

As such, there has been a fundamental shift in how military families are afforded housing. No longer supplied by base administrators and military personnel, domestic military housing is now arranged through private developers and housing management corporations, and these arrangements are long-term, with 50-year leases on land and contracts for maintenance and management (US Government Accountability Office, 2018b, p. 1). Along the way, the military has conveyed ownership of more than 200,000 housing units to private corporations. To bolster this initiative, it fronted $3.4 billion to undertake renovations in 52,000 homes, and supply seed capital for the construction of 80,000 new housing units (Pell, 2019b). Military families receive a Basic Allowance for Housing (BAH), which is then utilized as a payment stream for private development corporations to fund their operations and, of course, derive a profit. Along the way, contracts have been constructed with a series of 'incentive' payments, which are intended to reward the successful administration of housing. The intended result of these agreements, from the standpoint of the armed services, should be that military families gain a higher quality living experience.

However, if a 'spirit of partnership and patriotism' has driven corporate actors' involvement, it has not been especially evident in their build and maintenance outcomes. In 2018, *Reuters* news agency began to break a series of stories about widespread deplorable conditions in military housing and the deeply problematic behavior of those corporations responsible (Pell and Nelson, 2018). In response, during early 2019, the US Senate Armed Services Committee held hearings regarding the report of serious problems in military housing, inviting testimony of both tenants and development corporations. Senators heard reports of housing conditions that, by any interpretation, would not be considered acceptable, or even habitable. One tenant, turned activist, recited her experience with these reports across multiple bases:

> During my 2 years of research and advocacy, I received hundreds of reports from military families of mold growth, rodent and pest infestations, moisture intrusion, lead and asbestos exposures, radon concerns, base contamination, and cancer clusters in their housing. All of this was too often compounded by defensive, sometimes abusive housing staff (US Congress, Senate, 2018, p. 19).

Indeed, many of the stories emerging from hearings, reports, and extensive journalistic investigations reveal a pattern of systemic disregard for serious—often health-related—housing threats. These were not sporadic cases limited to one or two 'bad' bases, but widespread shortcomings in construction and maintenance across the country.

In fact, despite the veneer of shock and dismay exhibited by political, military and corporate actors, these problems should not have come as any real surprise. Certainly, at a local level, base officials across the country were receiving reports of deep structural and administrative problems in housing projects. Moreover, DOD's Office of the Inspector General (OIG) had already done inspection reports of military housing and base support services, and its findings should have been a warning bell for political actors and the military. In two separate reports, the OIG executed spot checks of 5 separate bases in the continental United States, two in the Washington, DC area, and three in the Southeast (US Department of Defense, Office of the Inspector General, 2015a, 2015b). Across these investigations, it identified 705 failures in military housing, including electrical, fire protection, and environmental health and safety deficiencies. Indeed, if domestic military housing and construction did not raise enough concern, an ensuing worldwide investigation of US military facilities and housing certainly should have.

> The DoD OIG issued six reports from July 2013 to July 2016 related to health and safety inspections of DoD facilities at various locations around the world, documenting 3,783 deficiencies in electrical system safety, fire protection systems, and environmental health and safety. During these inspections, the DoD OIG issued 12 notices of concern (NOCs), 7 detailing 319 critical deficiencies requiring immediate action at 24 of the 36 installations inspected (US Department of Defense, Office of the Inspector General, 2016, p. 3).

With the heightened level of Congressional concern directed at military contractors in contingency operations, especially in light of wastage in Afghanistan and Iraq, it seems inconceivable that either political actors or military officials remained blissfully unaware of what was going on in military bases across the country.

As in many cases of adaptive accumulation, the terms of transaction lie at the heart of the issue. Senatorial interrogators, along with critics of the Military's privatization initiative, raised the issue of 50-year contracts and weak incentives to change. Ultimately, these deal structures de-incentivize companies like Balfour Beatty, Corvias Group, or Lincoln Military Housing from investing in quality control and upkeep, while they instead pursue internal cost-control to get the lion's share of BAH and incentive payments. In 2019, the Army's OIG concluded that "base and incentive fees are not structured to provide RCI companies with significant performance incentives," and that, "incentive fee metrics were easily achieved and diminish the intent to incentivize higher standards of performance" (US Department of the Army, Office of the Inspector General, 2019, p. 10). The outcome of this was severe, as tenants at every inspected facility reported that they were being deceived and misled, with gross health and safety consequences for their families. Ultimately, they expressed a lack of faith in the motives and actions of those companies, as well as an awareness that oversight from military command was grossly lacking (Britzky, 2019). More severely, given the fact that military departments do not hold majority share in privatization partnerships, the room for participating corporations to obscure and with-hold relevant information remains large.

From the corporate end of this accumulative dynamic, companies have done everything in their political power to enhance returns. Corporations involved in housing initiatives have clearly undertaken weak construction and retrofitting of houses, manifested in the myriad problems emerging across the country. Harrowing as these tales are, the willingness to act has been greatly overshadowed by an instinct towards cost control and the attainment of incentive fees. Balfour Beatty kept two logbooks for maintenance records, one issued to military command, and one kept in secret, which showed the real state of repairs. In an undercover investigation of Tinker Air Force Base,

> Balfour Beatty, among the U.S. military's largest housing providers, systematically falsified ... maintenance logs for years .... The fake entries made the company appear responsive to tenant complaints and unsafe conditions, helping it secure millions in "performance incentive fees" for good service that it otherwise often would not have qualified for. The efforts left families in harm's way and persuaded Air Force brass to ignore warnings of trouble raised by military base employees (Pell, 2019b, para.6).

In fact, work orders on housing have been regularly 'massaged', in order to meet quotas that trigger incentive fees. Altered records turned out to be more widespread than initially understood, as employees have come forward from multiple sites to register the pressure they felt to alter completion rates for repairs. One employee articulated this pressure succinctly: "You either make these numbers match so we can get the incentive fees, or you may not have a job tomorrow," adding that. "We fudged the numbers, and even now it's not easy to say that" (Pell, 2019a, para.7).

Importantly, employees and local base officials reported these systematic misdeeds to no avail, as the coordinating unit, the Air Force Civil Engineering Center, regularly chose to smooth relations with its private developers. Ultimately, the institutional voice that should have had regulatory oversight simultaneously held responsibility to promote development of private housing (Pell, 2019b). In such problematic regulatory environments, the opening for adaptive accumulation is large, and corporate players enjoy wide latitude for their actions. In the report issued by the Army OIG, there was a clear indication of problematic oversight and confusion. Citing the military's imperative to prioritize "operating force over generating force," the report points to a severe reduction in oversight personnel (US Department of the Army, Office of the Inspector General, 2019, p. 10). This 'risk management' resulted in the removal of local command from most authority and oversight, a centralization of fiscal disbursements, and the prohibition of health and welfare inspections. In addition, compliance has been generated only through information provided by the companies involved—an obvious red flag, given the manipulation of maintenance and repair figures. Even with the best of intentions, the Army OIG found that roles and responsibilities of station commanders, garrison commanders, and base housing staff were unclear in terms of authority and responsibility (2019, pp. 5, 10). In the end, military officials were simply unable or unwilling to measure or control the activity of companies involved in the housing initiatives. More ominously, Senatorial hearings clearly revealed a perception of retribution being directed at those tenants stepping forward to complain to military command.

On an issue as sensitive as military family housing, it is odd that it took a media shaming for either Congressional or military figures to take notice. It is unclear whether, in the long run, the military has saved revenues, but it has certainly paid dearly in terms of public trust and quality of life for its personnel. Congressional actors, of course, have reacted in an appropriately 'stern' manner, reminding participating companies what is at stake. In a manner representative of other Senators, Kirsten Gillibrand reprimanded testifying CEOs that they should, "believe this is not just an opportunity to make money. [That] there is nothing wrong with making money in this capitalist society of ours, but it is also an opportunity to serve the men and women in the military … and their families" (US Congress, Senate, 2018, p. 89). Ensuing legislation has been directed at stepping up oversight and enforcement, laying the groundwork for a Tenants' Bill of Rights, which would be procured by DOD. As DOD produced such guidelines in early 2020, they came under immediate scrutiny for omitting three critical components: right to inspection history; right to withhold rent payment; and dispute resolution. The reasoning for this became clear soon enough, as defense officials anonymously revealed they were "protecting the financial interest of the bond-holders themselves … reconciling how … to implement it so that the lenders can be comfortable with it, effectively" (Britzky, 2020, para.5). At the same time, participating corporations have also pushed back, arguing that the real problem is below-market payment rates. A representative of Corvias Group made exactly such claims in front of a Congressional subcommittee, suggesting that BAH is not keeping pace with market rates (US Congress, House, 2020). In other words, despite having revealed strong profits among all participating corporations in the previous year, there is now a move to re-construct the entire problem as a function of underfunding on long-term government contracts. So, while these corporations have no choice but to respond to the sudden criticism emanating from Congress, they can be expected to 'pivot', by recasting their negligence through a demand for the renegotiation (and betterment) of the funding terms for their 'patriotic' service.

3.5 Conclusion

This chapter has made the case that corporate relationships to the US military extend well beyond the weapons procurement process. Across this increasingly complex web of contracts, corporate actors have been able to secure extensive private revenues from public budgets, and this occurs on a repetitive and long-term basis. Their insertion into semi-public roles affords them both a structural security and ideological cover in their quest for returns. Once insinuated into the military planning process, whether providing mission infrastructure or delivering electricity to military housing, such contracts cannot be easily sidestepped or eliminated. Public institutions typically take time to assemble—or re-assemble—large-scale capacities, so the disruption of contracts would render a void in services that would be politically and practically untenable. This fact is especially well understood by those firms holding large-scale contracts, enabling them to push the boundaries of their relationship with government, even during moments of public scandal. Congressional members may intermittently express outrage over the well-being of the nation's troops and their families, but they know well that DOD capacity, across a large, expensive public institution, is deeply and inextricably wound up in accumulative dynamics of private actors —a reality unlikely to change anytime soon.

Chapter 4: Health, Healthcare, and Adaptive Accumulation

Besides finance, there is only one arena that rivals the politico-economic significance of the military in the US, and that is the health sector. This sector forms one the largest and most opportune areas for profit, given both its universal and its immediate necessity to individual and societal well-being. The boundaries of this market also appear immanently expandable, as limits on what properly constitutes 'sufficient' health or health provision remain hard to define. In the U.S., perhaps not surprisingly, the allure of health as a market commodity has proven considerably stronger than in its comparable national counterparts. But even in America, broad health coverage requires the organizing mechanism of government, such that the greatest degree of protection is extended to the widest segment of population possible. Healthcare, in other words, does not spontaneously emerge, but must be fostered through public policy that effectively promotes and maintains health across the population.

In countries where governments have *entirely* taken over this public objective, including both the purchasing and provision of healthcare, the term 'universal care' is properly utilized. There are, however, few examples of true universal care, as most systems mix public forms of payment and provision with private ones, in order to achieve a total universal, usually highly regulated, effect. Historically, US public policy has probably veered the furthest away from universal care, and with tens of millions of US citizens either still going without healthcare or grossly underinsured, it is typically understood as an outlier among advanced industrial states. In fact, public healthcare expansion in the United States has proceed mostly in fits and starts, stemming back to the administration of Theodore Roosevelt and culminating in the awkward compromise of the Affordable Care Act (ACA) of 2010. Alongside this process, however, there has also been a marked explosion in profitability of healthcare delivery, along with the growth of the largest healthcare market in the world. Indeed, it has been estimated that by 2026, this market will constitute a full 20 percent of US GDP (Himmelstein *et al.*, 2018, p. 9).

The concurrence of these trends is not accidental. This chapter makes the case that the increasing entwinement between a growing private sector and an ongoing patchwork of political reforms has rendered a health system that not only maximizes private involvement but is now highly conducive to adaptive ac-

---

Note: Sections of this chapter have been adapted from: Loeppky (2019).

https://doi.org/10.1515/9783110761801-004

cumulation. Payers and providers alike have positioned themselves at the cross-roads between public policy objectives, a complicated health system, contradictory government largesse, and the expansion of private revenue streams. It has become a truism to state that the healthcare system in the U.S. is unnecessarily disjointed, complicated and costly, but there are, tellingly, no lobbies among its constituent parts that wish to see it otherwise. And it is precisely the governmental attempts to address these shortcomings, without fundamentally changing the structure of delivery, that now offer up the greatest possibilities for market entry and expansion, all with the ideological cover of pursuing public good and beneficiaries' well-being.

While our purpose cannot be a full exposé of US health and healthcare, the chapter hits on significant historical moments, as well as critical components, of the health system, in order to lay bare the profitable aims of industry actors that are now embedded in publicly generated health programs. It begins with a short history of health reform in the U.S., providing background to the current structural parameters of healthcare delivery. Rather than a detailed history, the goal is to map out landmark evolutionary moments that have laid the groundwork for the explosion of public-private interactions in the contemporary era. Following this, a more detailed consideration of component parts of US health delivery provides a window into the peculiar accumulative dynamics of the health sector. These include: 1) the creation and long-term growth of the privately administered Medicare Advantage program; 2) the establishment and growth of Medicare's prescription drug coverage through the Medicare Modernization Act of 2003; and 3) the passage and ongoing fate of the ACA, particularly its expansion and subsidization of the commercial insurance market. The chapter then closes with a discussion of healthcare prospects in the wake of the Trump administration and its failed attempts to dismantle the ACA, either through legislation or by unravelling its component parts.

4.1 US Health Reform Through the Twentieth Century

It is often noted that US health carries with it a profound paradox: the country that leads the advanced industrial world in health technology also administers one of its least effective health delivery systems. By almost any measure, the US healthcare system is in an overall state of disarray. It costs more than any other health system, with a 2019 (pre-COVID) *per capita* spending of $11,072, amounting to a whopping 17.1% of GDP (OECD, 2021a). This is roughly twice as much the average in other OECD countries. Worse still, the US system does not bring about the health outcomes purported by its advocates. Prior to implementation of the ACA, some 52 million were without healthcare, with another 34 million understood as underinsured (with out-of-pocket costs acting as an impediment to care) (Rao and Hellander, 2014, p. 216). Even following the rollout of the ACA, some 27–28 million remained uninsured, with another 50 million-plus experiencing underinsured status (Waitzkin and Hellander, 2016, p. 1). And most damning are outcome indicators (mortality, life expectancy, infant mortality, mental health, etc.), which place US healthcare definitively low on the list among its peer countries (OECD, 2019).

In the end, there is simply no empirical evidence—indeed, there is copious evidence to the contrary—that market-based healthcare systems (especially insurance) are anything but detrimental to populations. The reasons for this have been reviewed in more depth elsewhere, but the singular most important issue is the impossibility of price leverage in a free-ranging myriad of payers (Loeppky, 2014, pp. 69–70). Payers and providers have always been divided in the U.S., both from each other and amongst themselves. As such, no payer possesses the structural leverage to have a meaningful impact on the prices paid for healthcare provision, and providers enjoy a unique capacity to charge for goods and services at levels far above other countries. This combines with the politico-economic reality that health and healthcare are treated, in both corporate and political domains, as a form of industrial and economic development, rendering market prices (and profits) that continue to climb faster than anywhere else. In much of the early history of reform attempts, it was mostly providers—physicians and hospitals—that formed the greatest barrier to change. By the close of the millennium, however, opposition had spread to multiple corners, crushing reform attempts and resulting in a highly divided, complicated, and very costly system of health delivery.

Early in the twentieth century, hospitals were run for the poor by charitable organizations and medical costs were paid for entirely out-of-pocket (Berkowitz, 2010, p. 3). Efforts at reform included an attempt to create medical coverage for workers in moments of disability, led by the American Association for Labour Legislation. Although opposed by the American Federation of Labour, it managed to garner grassroots support in key states, the most prominent of which was New York. In that state, a 1919 bill supporting health insurance passed the state Senate, but was shut down in the House by the Speaker and a host of lobbying interests, including physicians, hospitals, and insurance companies (Hoffman, 2010, p. 1541).

The lobbying power of providers only grew in the wake of the depression and the emergence of social legislation in the New Deal era. The American Medical Association (AMA) recoiled at the prospect of government organized change in healthcare, fearing the regulation of fees and lowered income for physicians, and its consistent mobilization during this period sabotaged any chance of health reform. The proposed inclusion of health reform within the Social Security Act of 1935 was abandoned, after it became clear that physicians' opposition would likely derail the entire bill. Even after Franklin Delano Roosevelt's re-election in 1936, the administration was still not able to find political currency for such reform, and Congressional figures, lobbied by the AMA, indicated that they would shut down any attempts at legislation (Starr, 2013, pp. 46–48). Similarly, the Truman administration's support for national insurance was blocked in every conceivable way by a Congress heavily influenced by providers' lobbying efforts. Public debate was steered toward a fear of 'socialized medicine', and the possibilities for change were pre-emptively closed down. Interestingly, in an early bid to grow the health sector as an industry, however, Congress did support legislation that boosted the infrastructural capacities of providers, through "programs that Truman proposed for aid for hospital construction and medical research, which substantially increased investment in technologically intensive medical services" (2013, p. 50).

Only in the 1960s did meaningful policy reform emerge, but only for selective parts of the US population. The advent of Medicare and Medicaid in 1965 established almost universal purchasing of healthcare for US citizens over the age of 65, covering hospital care (Medicare Part A), physician and home care (Medicare Part B), and a federally-backed but state-administered program for the poor (Medicaid). Arguably, these programs were a victory for the private healthcare market, because they extended care to those segments of the population who were the most vulnerable and in need of care, but also the least profitable (Hacker, 2002, p. 290). The remainder of the covered population received their benefits mostly *via* employment-based health plans, administered by private actors. For many involved in the adoption of Medicare, the long-term goal had been its extension to the entire US population, with an eye to overcoming the resistance of the AMA, the health insurance industry, myriad providers, and the bulk of Republicans (Berkowitz, 2017, pp. 522–526). This would prove unattainable in a health landscape dominated by private players, and even Medicare as the beachhead of single-payer care has become significantly vulnerable to the accumulation strategies of corporate actors.

As the strength and complexity of private coverage and provision in the US grew, the failed Clinton health reform of the early 1990s stands as a watershed moment. It formed the political experience from which subsequent reforms would be shaped, clearly demonstrating both the dominance of market actors and the power of political figures resistant to equitable healthcare coverage. By the 1990s, healthcare costs had long since become unmanageable in the U.S., with the rising costs of coverage now felt by large corporations supplying health benefits, and the dilemma of uninsured Americans reaching catastrophic proportions (Béland and Waddan, 2010, p. 219). With the Democrats' electoral victory in 1992, the potential for healthcare reform seemed real enough, and the Clinton administration mustered an alliance of stakeholders, specifically large corporations, to drive healthcare change. Getting major corporations onside offered the chance to nudge other players in the healthcare domain to adopt reforms—a strategic move that, while successful at first, proved to be the Achilles heel of the Clinton reforms.

The backing of corporate actors in the pursuit of coverage for the working population did not signal a changing political culture, so much as an indication that these actors wanted to cut costs related to their own health plans (Swenson and Greer, 2002). The wider health industry quickly understood the 'harmful' political situation, wherein any call for greater government involvement would potentially signal external price controls, and a reining in of very profitable revenue streams. As such, pharmaceutical and health maintenance organizations (HMOs) worked individually with major corporate actors to reduce, or at least stabilize, prices, for the time being. This immediately undermined the publicly stated basis for reforms—making US corporations competitive—and brought a wave of resistance from foes and, eventually, existing corporate allies. The Health Security Act, the legislative expression of Clinton's 'managed competition' (mandating expanded employer-based health insurance), was intensely resisted by Republicans, while the insurance, pharmaceutical, and small business lobbies forcefully denounced it (Béland and Waddan, 2010, pp. 220 – 221). In this field of hostility, hitherto corporate allies failed to back the administration, as they now perceived themselves as having successfully negotiated better terms for their healthcare coverage on the open market (Giaimo and Manow, 1999, p. 989). This would prove to be misguided, as provision prices across-the-board began to rise as soon as the 'threat' of government intervention collapsed. Politically, the effects of this reform failure cannot be understated: the space for broad healthcare reform disintegrated, and it would remain extremely limited for almost two decades. During this time, the health industry consolidated and expanded its presence in US society, with the deep entrenchment of market-based healthcare, along with all of its accompanying challenges.

4.2 Adapting the Component Parts of US Healthcare

As the growing ranks of the uninsured meant relatively fewer paying beneficiaries, and as growing premium prices could not compensate for this finite consumer base, actors within the health industry have since sought out strategies to underwrite an expansionary business model. This has not happened all at once, but rather in piecemeal form. Industrial players have capitalized on moments of incremental healthcare reform in a manner that elevates their public prominence within health delivery but optimizes their potential for politically-secured profit streams. Health, in this sense, follows the model of adaptive accumulation, insofar as corporate actors seek to translate a share of secure public funding into revenues, supplying federal programs with sanctioned market purchasing and provision. This results in high-cost/high-profit markets that are relatively insulated, because any increased instability in delivery can have damning political consequences. This gives corporate actors considerable leverage over government action, including demands that 'predictability' be built into these public-private arrangements over the long-term. Any attempt to alter these conditions meets with voracious resistance.

What follows is an exploration of this dynamic through various components of US healthcare delivery, investigating both their origins and contemporary features, in order to shed light on the adaptive arrangements secured by market players. While not an exhaustive picture of US health delivery, it supplies a representative snapshot of the political dynamics that have furnished highly profitable public-private relationships. And while the U.S. is hardly the only country to utilize such relationships in the health sector, its government actors demonstrate a particular willingness to reproduce conditions that render extraordinary market returns.

4.2.1 Transforming Medicare

Following the downfall of the Clinton reform, one thing remained clear in US health: policy reform that interfered with, rather than bolstered, market presence in purchasing and delivery would be viewed unfavourably.[1] The result was stepped-up competition between insurance companies and HMOs to tap into the existent but still lucrative health domains. As Andrew Kelly (2016) has correctly identified, this created market pressure to find new sources of revenue in a tightening field of expensive premiums.

> Increasing commercial penetration also sparked competition between [managed care organizations, or MCOs] that had spillover effects into the Medicare market. As the employer-sponsored insurance market became saturated, MCOs turned to Medicare for new sources of revenue. In the fight for beneficiaries, insurers offered richer and richer benefit

---

1 This section is a modified version of Loeppky (2019, pp. 737–742).

packages, as well as lower cost sharing, in order to win the Medicare market—even if that meant incurring short-run losses (2016, p. 331).

Indeed, in a move not unlike the one exercised later by mortgage lenders, 'teaser rates' were offered to entice beneficiaries into private Medicare arrangements (2016, p. 331). The move to utilize the public, single-payer structure of Medicare as means to realize private revenue streams started in the 1980s, expanded in the late 1990s and was consolidated in the 2000s. This was not an unintended consequence, but rather an industry-driven strategy in the face of both tightening markets and the irresistibility of adaptive accumulation strategies.

The very possibility of private Medicare plans emerged with the passage of the 1982 Tax Equity and Fiscal Responsibility Act (TEFRA), which allowed private plans to change the terms of their plans outside of the boundaries set by traditional Medicare (TM) fee-for-service (FFS) coverage (Hacker, 2004, p. 253). Plans could now pull in guaranteed government paid premiums and arrange their risk pools in a manner that corresponded with profitability. Later, under the Clinton administration, pressured by a Republican Congress, privately administered Medicare surged upward. The Balanced Budget Act (BBA) of 1997 formalized this process, by naming the program (Medicare+Choice) and recognizing its increasing significance and value in seniors' health provision. Indeed, it even formally enshrined such plans as 'Part C' of the Medicare program.

At the same time, in an era of government austerity, the BBA sought to rein in the costs of public programs generally, and Medicare payments would be no exception. It attempted to reduce payments to private plans, recognizing that the growth in Medicare+Choice plans had accelerated substantially. The formula for payments to private insurance plans, most of them HMOs, had awarded considerable advantages to insurers, who could take in the guaranteed premiums while lowering their overall payments to beneficiaries. With a payout of premiums set at 95% of TM rates, adjusted for demographics and regional data, insurers could actively select the counties that attracted the highest reimbursement and lowest cost outlays—a classic case of adverse selection (McGuire, Newhouse and Sinaiko, 2011). As such, the BBA directed the Center for Medicare and Medicaid Services (CMS) to apply refined risk adjustment against its payments, based on beneficiaries' diagnoses. Paying more for sicker populations and reducing payments for healthier populations hit the mark—between 1997 and 2003, over 2 million seniors would be involuntarily withdrawn from Part C plans (2011, pp. 309–312). Even Congress' attempt to remedy the situation for insurers in 1999 could not overcome this trend, as risk adjustment bit into the lucrative business of selective seniors' healthcare.

With the Republican Bush administration, this situation would not be allowed to stand, as it urged passage of the Medicare Modernization Act (MMA). Best known for its drug benefit, discussed below, the MMA also recast the Medicare+Choice program as 'Medicare Advantage' (MA) and aimed to enhance its attractiveness to the health industry. Payment rates were boosted to 100 percent of risk adjusted fee-for-service rates, and reached much higher *de facto* levels. Indeed, it was the intent of the administration to encourage private plans, by providing more generous payment structures for those beneficiaries willing to convert to Part C arrangements. Following the MMA, the extraordinary growth of this program became impossible to ignore, and it now constitutes 33 percent of all Medicare plans. The major insurers—Humana, UnitedHealth, Cigna—have very substantial stakes in this market, and industry lobbyists defend these interests vociferously. Accordingly, congressional lobbying in this specific sector has grown dramatically to circumvent or modify any legislation that might affect payment rates to industry (Kelly, 2016, p. 336).

The insurance industry's ability to lock in profitable streams has been reflected in the political leverage afforded to those controlling large beneficiary markets. With some 19 million enrollees, the industry's stability and well-being has become a matter of necessity in political circles.

> The structure of Medicare policy ... gives [MCOs] the responsibility for the direct provision of a public good that is, quite literally, a matter of life and death to US seniors. This provides MCOs with significant and increasing policy leverage ... With the benefit of a longer time horizon, we see that the insurance industry is, in fact, able to draw considerable power and defensive sway from its bipartisan influence. MCOs can withdraw from participating in MA, they can withdraw from certain counties, or they can charge higher premiums or offer modified benefits to the millions of seniors enrolled in their plans, the potential effect of which is to throw a growing portion of the Medicare market into turmoil, forcing some beneficiaries to reenroll in traditional Medicare, purchase Medigap, find new private plans, and potentially face higher costs. The extent of the potential disruption, and therefore the political cost, caused by plan withdrawals or reductions increases with each new enrollee (2016, p. 337).

In keeping with adaptive accumulation, this means that industrial players utilize a 'public provider' persona to render the bloated payment structure relatively untouchable. Health, as with most other arenas of social policy, presents a conundrum: once private provision reaches a critical mass of participation, every regulation, modification or altercation (with, say, insurers) presents the strong possibility for political pain.

In an environment where industry possesses this kind of political leverage, corporate players are able to maneuver through regulatory constraints that might otherwise tamp down their profit expectations. CMS has long advocated the removal of MA payment incentives, and regulatory structures have surely been put in place to achieve such goals.[2] For instance, the abovementioned system of risk-adjustment has become increasingly refined, in order to remove imbalances between public and private coverage scenarios.[3] Under this ever-evolving method, insurers must assign hierarchical condition categories (HCCs) to each beneficiary, and CMS uses this information to assign a quantified risk score based on their demographic and health status. This risk score "represents the expected difference in spending for each Medicare beneficiary relative to spending for an FFS beneficiary with average risk" (Hayford and Burns, 2018, p. 2). A singular risk score for each insurance pool is then assigned to corporate bids to the MA program each year. CMS determines how payments to plans (usually determined at the county level) will be risk-adjusted against a benchmark FFS payment structure—higher payments for higher risk individuals, lower risk for lower risk individuals.

How can the insurance industry adapt and still profit in such a carefully regulated payment structure? The answer is two-fold. First, while the industry is not allowed to reject applications for MA, even for those with long-term, chronic conditions, it is still able to choose the geographic regions in which it offers coverage, as well as the structure of that coverage. Literature on advantageous selection suggests that MA attracts considerably healthier beneficiaries, and even since the stepped-up risk-adjustment formulas of MMA, with an increasingly severe 'lock-in' period applied to MA enrollees, mixed evidence exists as to whether risk selection has been mitigated (Brown *et al.*, 2014; Newhouse *et al.*, 2015). It is certainly the case that beneficiaries with chronic conditions or in need of acute care tend to gravitate back to conventional Medicare. Unlike the TM model, MA plans are based on care networks, and beneficiary care is restricted within those networks. As such, potential beneficiaries with complex, chronic conditions that require extensive specialist care tend to 'self-select' into TM, resulting in healthier risk pools for MA. Exploring long-term care, nursing care, and acute in-patient care, Momatazur Rahman *et al.* (2015) have suggested "that beneficiaries who report poorer health, use more health services,

---

2 The political imperative to do this has also long been established in both the cry for cost control, as well as the ever-ready argument (mostly in Republican circles) for 'voucherizing' Medicare (Oberlander, 2014).

3 This is not without precedent. In Germany, risk adjustment (*Riskostrukturausgleich*) has been utilized to ensure that insurance funds supply equal quality care and that premiums remain broadly egalitarian. However, this occurs in a context where funds operate on a non-profit basis, and the compulsion to undermine or maneuver around such risk adjustment is considerably more restrained (Loeppky, 2014, ch.5).

and have higher healthcare spending are more likely than their counterpart Medicare Advantage beneficiaries to leave Medicare Advantage plans" (2015, p. 1680). Risk adjustment *should* have strongly mitigated against selection, and it *should* have had the effect of equalizing payments for services between MA and TM. However, by 2009, the average overpayment to MA amounted to somewhere between 12% and 14%, totaling $12 billion in yearly additional costs for the Medicare program (McGuire, Newhouse and Sinaiko, 2011, p. 319).

A second and related path to adaptive accumulation involves coding practices. HCC categories are immensely complex, accounting for demographics, region, diagnostic classes, and aggregated individual health data. But the application of HCC under risk adjustment has not been negative for corporate actors. According to Brown and colleagues (2014),

> ... before risk adjustment MA plans fished in a pond of relatively healthy enrollees with little cost variance. Risk adjustment allows them to fish in a pond of enrollees who have higher costs on average but also highly variable costs. Indeed, we find that after risk adjustment, overpayments are higher, an increase equal to roughly 9% of average Medicare per capita spending (2014, p. 3338).

On the whole, risk adjustment brings more reward than costs, and substantial evidence suggests that, as beneficiaries enroll in MA, their diagnostic information is 'upcoded' to include conditions that attract greater payment to MA insurers. A Congressional Budget Office paper demonstrated that a switch to MA brings, on average, an increase in risk scores—a practice that has intensified over the life of the HCC risk adjustment scheme. Risk scores rose instantly 5.3% among those who switched from TM to MA in 2008, increasing to a figure of 8.0% in 2012. Additionally, the scores of these same individuals continued to rise at a subsequent yearly rate of 1.2% (Kronick, 2017, pp. 321–322). Overall, it is difficult to escape the conclusion that corporate players in this terrain have deftly navigated the regulatory criteria of 'risk' to deliver public programs in a manner that enhances payout and structured revenue.

For its part, the Obama administration recognized overpayment to MA programs as a drain on public revenue and an undermining element of equitable Medicare delivery. As part of the ACA, the President signaled his administration's intention to "... eliminate billions in unwarranted subsidies to insurance companies in the Medicare Advantage program—giveaways that boost insurance company profits but don't make you any healthier" (quoted in Volsky, 2014). Specifically, the legislation sought to pull back the perks enjoyed by industry within MA over its TM counterpart, by adding increased risk adjustment modifiers, changing the structure of benchmark payments, and rolling out taxes that affected MA.

These measures should have had pronounced and rapid effects but were instead subjected to the political pressure of widespread industrial intervention. From the outset, America's Health Insurance Plans (AHIP), the premier lobby for U.S. health insurers, made clear that "reimbursement reductions could drastically reduce enrollment in Medicare Advantage and disrupt plan offerings" (Jennings, 2015, p. np). Their lobbying efforts applied maximum pressure to both legislative and executive arms of government, and the returns were substantial. Under intense pressure from industry and Republican political opposition, the Obama administration soon announced the Quality-Based Bonus Payments Program (QBP), rapidly expanding a small quality incentive program built into the legislation. In the original program, insurance plans with a 4- or 5-star rating received a 1.5% bonus on their benchmark payments, but QBP extended this bonus to 3- and 3.5-star plans, awarding them a 3% and 3.5% payment bonus, respectively. And 4- and 5-star plans would now receive 4 and 5% benchmark payment increases. The impact of this 3-year program was large, exceeding $8 billion, and it amounted to a clear transitional subsidy for the insurance sector. As Kelly (2016) has pointed out, the administration's support "contradicted its own earlier policy declarations, opened itself up to criticism, and gave back a significant source of early funding for its signature legislative achievement" (2016, p. 342).

Beyond backdoor compensation, there have also been yearly policy reversals. The legislation was constructed to curb excess payments by freezing them at 2010 levels and then imposing incremental cuts from 2012 onward. The aim was to equalize reimbursement so that it would match TM rates, but also to recover some $156 billion in revenues over 10 years—funds that could be used to bolster other elements of healthcare reform. In early 2013, CMS made good on implementation by issuing advance notice on a proposed 2014 benchmark payment reduction of 2.3% (Book, 2013). However, when the final payment rates were issued months later, a not-so-surprising reversal had occurred, as a payment rate increase of 3.3% was finalized for 2014. This 5.6% upward adjustment would continue over the next 6 years. The results in Table 2 demonstrate a clear trend, in which CMS has been subject to industrial and political pressure to continue increasing benchmark payments to MA. Following the first advance notice of payment cuts in 2013, AHIP initiated an aggressive advertising campaign to depict the administration as threatening seniors' healthcare, along with a stepped-up lobbying effort on Capitol Hill (Haberkorn and Norman, 2013). Having won the results it needed in 2013, ensuing years brought pre-emptive interventions by industry, no longer waiting for advance notice and keeping the pressure on both Congress and the White House to adhere to rate increases (Norman, 2014).

Table 2: Percentage of Proposed and Final Adjustment Payment Rates to Medicare Advantage (2013 – 2019)

Year	Proposed (percent)	Final (percent)
2013 – 2014	-2.3	+3.3
2014 – 2015	-1.9	+0.4
2015 – 2016	-0.95	+3.2
2016 – 2017	+1.35	+0.85
2017 – 2018	+2.75	+2.95
2018 – 2019	+1.84	+3.4

Sources: (Millman, 2014; Ellison, 2015, 2016; Kelly, 2016; Morse, 2017; Porter, 2018).

In the end, the Obama Administration and the ACA did not make good on the promise to rein in MA program spending. The capacity of industry to secure accumulation streams from a public revenue source has proven both effective and unrelenting. Not only has this industry strategically grown this sector to a point that can be defended as politically sensitive, but the expected de-enrollment of seniors following the passage of the ACA simply has not come to pass. Industrial players can and have translated their quasi-public role into leverage associated to some 20 million voting citizens, all the while using that same leverage to frustrate cost control aspirations of CMS officials. The utilization of market choice in Medicare—originally intended to infuse 'efficiency'—has been largely successful in converting public use into private gain.

4.2.2 Drugs, US Seniors, and Medicare

The fostered growth of Medicare Advantage was only one outcome of the MMA—a lesser known element of the legislation at the time of its passage.[4] The bill's centerpiece was, in fact, a somewhat unexpected Republican-led effort to enlarge Medicare, by adding a drug benefits program, since known as Medicare Part D (MpD). On the face of it, this did not fit norm of US politics. The Bush Administration had emerged in the aftermath of an austere period of Congressional budgeting, and large portions of the Republican party were ideologically and politically against expanded government intervention or spending (save for De-

---

4 This is a modified version of Loeppky (2019, pp. 742–746).

fense spending). Indeed, there was little incentive on the part of GOP members to join in the political project, and their public testimonials made this clear. Republican Jeff Flake (AZ) expressed a broadly felt conservative skepticism towards the legislation: "I didn't come here to expand government like that. It will be a middle-class entitlement that will run away from us" (quoted in Jaenicke and Waddan, 2006, p. 221). In other words, ideological preferences do not explain MpD. Its ultimate ascension to law must account for adaptive accumulation, because MpD is custom-built for industrial advantage and securing long-term drug profits.

By the outset of 2000, the question of drug pricing had become critical in the US, particularly for seniors. Drugs were the fastest growing component of healthcare costs, and Medicare beneficiaries were among the most vulnerable to this cost escalation. The Democrats had long since incorporated a Medicare drug program into their party platform, and the drug re-importation question had put the issue front and center for one of the strongest lobbies in Washington (Harris, 2003).[5] As political pressure for the drug benefit was growing, the Pharmaceutical and Research Manufacturers of America (PhRMA) went into overdrive, attempting to optimize the outcome for the drug industry. PhRMA supported over 600 lobbyists during this period, and it doubled its lobbying budget to this end. In this sense, the lobbying that led to beneficial clauses in the MMA should not merely be seen as the defensive reactions of an industry. Instead, it should be viewed as a progressive strategy of accumulative logic. Republicans uncharacteristically enlarged an entitlement program not as political benevolence or compassion, but rather as part of an opportunity to adapt Medicare to greater profit potential.

> The MMA afforded an array of groups, many of whom had unrequited agendas deferred by past Medicare cost-containment efforts, an extraordinary opportunity to pursue their aims with $400 billion on the table—a pursuit made easier by the desire of both the Bush administration and Congress to expand the private sector in Medicare … A unified government under Democratic Party control would likely not have been *as generous* to providers, pharmaceutical companies, and private insurers (Oberlander, 2007, p. 198 emphasis added).

Importantly, 'privatization' does not capture this precisely, because the aim was not to privatize but to rearrange the largest single-payer health system in the

---

5 The controversy around drug re-importation crystallized in the early 2000s, when increasingly organized seniors groups in northern states chartered buses for prescription drug-buying trips to Canada. Online pharmacies in Canada soon began facilitating this market, and events reached crisis proportions for the drug industry when several US governors publicly questioned whether re-importation could not be used to lower their state Medicaid costs.

world. Rearrangement here means locking in revenue streams without removing existing—or discouraging new—government involvement in drug acquisition.

As a single-payer system, Medicare has always existed in a tense peace with private providers. As the largest payer for healthcare in the US (44 million enrollees in 2017), it certainly retains the potential to utilize its position for price leverage. This is, of course, the advantage that most state-organized or state-run healthcare systems have in the face of rising provider costs. With universal purchasing, there is only one buyer, and healthcare providers may negotiate with this buyer but ultimately are left to "take it or leave it." In the US system, especially in relation to the drug industry, this has never been the case. Purchasers are divided up between multiple parties, and no one party possesses enough leverage to exert strong downward pressure on drug prices. This has meant that pharmaceutical prices are, by a considerable margin, the most expensive in the advanced industrial world, as Figure 1 makes abundantly clear.

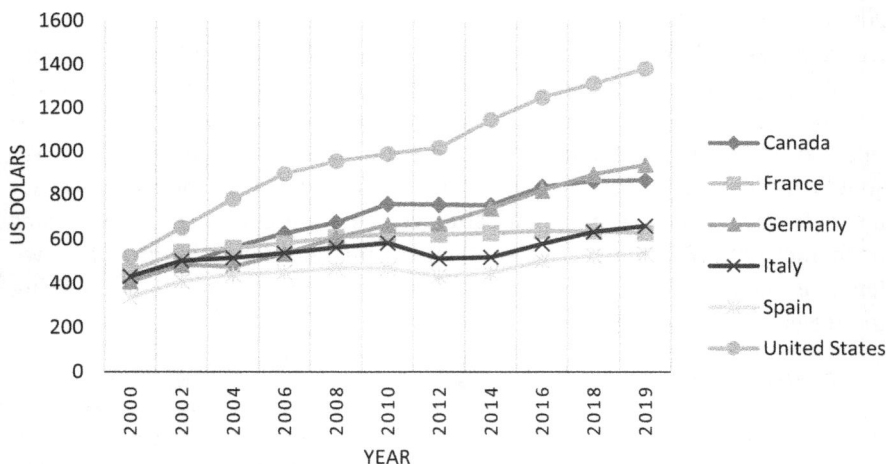

Figure 1: Per capita Pharmaceutical Spending by Country, 2000–2019, Source: (OECD, 2021b).

The worldwide drug industry is immensely profitable, and the US market for drugs is, by far, the most important element of this profitability. As such, the proposed expansion of government involvement in drug acquisition offered both possibility and danger. As the Veterans Administration (VHA) healthcare plan had already demonstrated, government leverage over this market (and provision in general) could have resounding (downward) price effects. The MMA, therefore, became the vehicle not only to defend existing market practices, but also grow them in ways that would boost rather than detract from profitability. As the legislation took form, budgetary levels for prescription drug acquisition were set at $400 billion over a decade, an amount that was projected to cover one quarter of seniors' drug costs. This limited coverage was the result of the specific structure of the benefit, ostensibly aimed at balancing the obvious needs of seniors with the limited resources of the federal government—the latter having gone from surplus to deficit in the wake of immense tax cuts and major military spending in both Afghanistan and Iraq (Crystal, 2003). Its design included what infamously came to be known as the 'doughnut hole', wherein the federal government would reimburse 75 percent of beneficiaries' drug costs up to a stipulated level ($2250 in 2006) and resume payments only after 'catastrophic coverage' levels were exceeded ($5100 in 2006). This gap in coverage was designed to grow over time, with the coverage gap in 2018 tripping at $3750 and catastrophic coverage resuming at $8418 (The Kaiser Family Foundation, 2017). This front-loading of government subsidy offered an enhanced incentive for Medicare seniors to enroll in the MpD program, while it also exposed them to greater back-end, out-of-pocket costs in stepped-up drug coverage. From the outset, MpD used government revenues to supercharge the seniors' drug market while privatizing the lion's share of risk.

The upshot of this 'injection' into the prescription, generic and biological drug market is that it enlarged the market for sales. Unlike the MA program, which offered private plans as an option, MpD could *only* be administered by private drug plans (PDPs). This put the insurance industry in the driver's seat for plan administration, and it made the likelihood of serious cost control all but disappear. To reinforce this market security, the drug industry negotiated a clause within the MMA that prohibits Department of Human Health and Services (DHHS) from using its regulatory leverage to affect the pricing of drugs. Specifically, section 1860D-11(i) of the Social Security Act is amended, whereby the DHHS Secretary "(1) may not interfere with the negotiations between drug manufacturers and pharmacies and PDP sponsors; and (2) may not require a particular formulary or institute a price structure for the reimbursement of covered part D drugs" (US Congress, 2003, p. 2099). This is a remarkable clause, insofar as the government actually handcuffs itself with regard to the most useful tool related to drug policy sustainability. The results for industry, on the other hand, have been both considerable and worth defending. Spending in MpD has increased from $44.3 billion in 2006 to $92 billion in 2018, growing from 10.8 percent to 15.9 percent of Medicare spending. And this spending is projected to accelerate with a 4.7 percent annual growth rate until 2026, at which point it will constitute 17.5 percent of total Medicare spending (Hoadley, Cubanski and Neuman, 2015, pp. 1686–1687; The Kaiser Family Foundation, 2017). A 2015 study suggests that MpD pays at least double the OECD average for patented drugs; that it pays 73 percent more than Medicaid and 80 percent more than VHA for brand name drugs; and that utilizing the same Federal Supply Schedule as VHA would have saved MpD $16 billion a year (Gagnon, 2015). Not surprisingly, the role of MpD in total US prescription drug spending has increased substantially, growing from 18 percent of the market in 2006 to 29 percent in 2015 (with projected growth to 35 percent in 2025) (The Kaiser Family Foundation, 2019). Finally, the growing prominence of MpD spending is not a function of enhanced competition, as just five firms—United Health, Cigna, Aetna, CVS Health, and Express Scripts—control over two-thirds of the market (Hoadley, Cubanski and Neuman, 2016).

As in the case of Medicare Advantage, the ACA, in part, was intended as a vehicle to address the severity of drug spending in MpD. However, this was aimed at relieving the spending burden for consumers rather than addressing the structural effects of MpD on drug sales. The relevant sections of the legislation established progressively greater subsidies that would close the 'doughnut hole' by 2020, restoring the payment balance to a 75/25 covered/out-of-pocket balance. While there is no denying that this helps US seniors, surely a worthy goal, it also reinforces an already heavy personal cost across the *entire* drug benefit (up until catastrophic costs, over $8148 in 2018, after which enrollees pay 5 percent). Additionally, the ACA did impose a 50 percent manufacturers' rebate on the coverage gap, meaning that government subsidies will fill the 25 percent remainder by 2020. But no amount of countervailing subsidy or enforced rebates will address the issue of price escalation or the basic structure of MpD. There may be an ongoing debate over ACA coverage gap subsidies, but this is an ideological battle over *how much*, not whether or not, government should subsidize a market-adapted system (Roy, 2012; Osborn and Beier, 2017). There was certainly no proposal during the Obama administration to reintroduce serious government leverage into the negotiation of drug prices, as exists in most other OECD countries. In fact, on existing programs, the ACA more generally works to reinforce the status quo, while trying to soften its more difficult consequences for patients. As such, it allows MpD to continue as a vehicle for adaptive accumulation, paying a bigger portion of inflated US drug prices with public revenues, boosting insurance, pharmaceutical, and biopharmaceutical profits.

4.2.3 The Affordable Care Act

Nowhere has the adaptation of the health industry been more obvious than in the largest instance of healthcare reform since the passage of Medicare and Medicaid in 1965.[6] Just as the latter programs are properly understood as an accommodation of private market interests, so too can the ACA be seen as a reworking of the healthcare system, such that it remains conducive to commercial profits. The Clinton reform failure forestalled any large-scale political action on healthcare for 15 years, as political figures exhibited little appetite for the multipronged backlash that such action invites, but its haunting presence certainly remained. The plan's demise also established "the prime directive of [any future] health reform: do not disturb the existing insurance system and the already insured ... [and that] various formidable interests—insurers, employers, the medical care industry, and states were invested in the prevailing order" (Oberlander, 2016, pp. 804 – 805). Nonetheless, the Congressional Democratic electoral victories and the dramatic emergence of the Obama administration in 2008 opened a unique political window, in which the passage of meaningful healthcare reform presented itself as a rare opportunity.

This opportunity would take dramatic twists and turns, and the ACA would be born into a world of outright hostility and resistance, regardless of its tepid character and similarity to past Republican reform proposals (Starr, 2013, p. ch.7). While the ACA's largely Republican-driven political difficulties are considered below, the primary concern here is the way in which reform has been molded into an accommodating set of programs *vis-à-vis* market interests. With calls to make U.S. healthcare more inclusive, the health industry rallied around a new set of objectives: ensure that any Democratic reform stops short of full government administration or single-payer structure. This could only be achieved, however, with 'ahead of the curve' lobbying, ensuring that profitable corporate participation was part and parcel of reform. Along these lines, the prospect of systemic reform legislation could be seen as industrial opportunity rather than threat. Deftly lobbying the reform process, industrial actors structured their interests into the architecture of the ACA, ensuring the extensively fragmented state of U.S. healthcare was not only preserved but even extended.

For their part, the Obama administration and leading Democrats made sure to avoid decisions that would draw the fire of the health industry. Indeed, the *leitmotif* of the government negotiation process was corporatist-style deal making. The administration proved singularly adept at providing enticements that industry could not easily refuse. What John Geyman (2018) has labeled the administration's 'surrender-in-advance' strategy would bring onside all the major purchasers and providers of the health system. This began with the pharmaceutical and hospital industries, both of which sought reassurances of their position

---

6 This section is a modified version of Loeppky (2019, pp. 746 – 749).

in healthcare delivery. In early deals with the administration, wherein both industries pledged their political support and some resources, the administration surrendered far more valuable guarantees. The MMA's prohibition on government involvement in pricing or formularies was extended to the ACA, supplying extraordinary assurances for two industries responsible for the fastest rate of price increases. These industries' negotiating groups—PhRMA and the American Hospital Association (AHA)—were well aware that the benefits of a government-driven, enlarged healthcare market would translate into more patients/customers. As such, the "up-front concessions were substantial: They limited the law's ability to deliver tangible benefits to the middle class and largely took off the table tools of cost control used in other nations, such as provider rate-setting and government negotiation of drug prices" (Hacker, 2010, p. 865). As the aforementioned data for Medicare Part D makes clear, drug prices have accelerated under the ACA, particularly in recent years, and particularly in sought-after prescription drug classes (Norman and Karli-Smith, 2016).

While providers fared well under the ACA, the largest changes came for payers: insurance companies formed the backbone around which the legislation would be constructed and maintained. Represented by its umbrella organization, AHIP, the insurance industry followed a textbook version of adaptive accumulation: accept more government regulation; attune it as much as possible to assured revenue streams; and project a public purpose in doing so. As a result, the ACA is designed for minimal disruption of the existing insurance system while it extends coverage to the uninsured or under-insured. In order to do this, it expands eligibility for Medicaid (to 138 percent of the poverty line, dependent on state governments' participation in the program), but it also bolsters the individual insurance market for those without employment-based insurance or Medicaid support. It mandates state individual insurance 'exchanges' in which insurance companies offer accessible plans that meet federal criteria. These criteria, no doubt, softened some of the sharper edged elements of health insurance in the US. They addressed discrimination based on pre-existing conditions; extended coverage for dependent children; and eliminated the heinous practice of recission (Vick, 2009).[7] But the *quid-pro-quo* was also straightforward: if the industry was to expand its coverage to 'riskier' beneficiaries with less purchasing power, it demanded a strong 'individual mandate' that made the purchase of health insurance legally compulsive, with enforcement, expanding the pool of paying customers. Indeed, AHIP's stance on the emergent legis-

---

7 Recission is a retroactive cancellation of a health insurance policy, based on a review of the beneficiary's file and the conclusion that the insurer did not have complete information.

lation always revolved around the strength of this mandate. As Nelson Lichtenstein (2017) has rightly pointed out, the prospect of any real free market "worried
private insurers who ... feared that millions of young, healthy and/or low-income
people would pay [any weak] penalty and skip coverage. They wanted *more government regulation*, and a *stronger mandate*, not less" (2017, p. 127 emphasis
added).

At the same time, AHIP worked assiduously to position its corporate constituents as the leading beneficiaries of government largesse. For much of the debate surrounding the emergence of the ACA, there had been proposals for
some kind of public insurance option to compete on the exchange, with an
eye to keeping private plans honest and capturing unmet public need. This garnered industry's hostility, as officials argued they could not compete against an
insurer with the full backing of the US government. As such, while the possibility
of a government option was being entertained in the House of Representatives,
the full force of AHIP lobbying was brought to bear on the parallel Senate bill
that eventually would be the basis for legislative passage. Not only was the public option dropped from that bill, but government support was, in fact, directed
towards subsidies for private insurance premiums for individuals between 138
and 400 percent of the poverty line, as well as cost-sharing reduction payments
for insurance companies participating in the insurance exchanges (Levitt, Cox
and Claxton, 2017).

None of this is to presume that intervention into the insurance markets is
solely a governmental gift to industry—certainly, the expansion of healthcare
rolls by 16 – 20 million US citizens has merit, particularly for those receiving coverage for the first time. However, it does point to industrial strategies of both purchasers and providers that defend the complexity and fragmentation of US
healthcare delivery, with the aim of preserving—even expanding—its profoundly
accumulative nature. Ensuring this system of multiple divisions generates contracts never placed under any price leverage, allowing handsome profits
among purchasers and providers alike. In this sense, the continuing insistence
in US political circles that market organization delivers population-wide healthcare in a qualitatively superior and cost-effective form continues to reveal itself
as ideological servitude rather than evidence-based public policy recommenda-
tion (Waitzkin and Hellander, 2016, p. 16).

In the wake of the 2016 election, the ACA faced considerable uncertainty, as
populist, conservative and pro-market elements of the Republican right sought
an agreed upon path to repeal the law. Initial attempts resulted in failure, as
the proposed alternatives proved politically unpalatable and unsupported by
the powerful industrial sectors noted above. The strategic maneuvering here of
various sectors of the health industry, especially insurance, speak to their

uniquely adaptive disposition towards the ACA. AHIP's position on the final round of repeal attempts—the Graham-Cassidy repeal bill—summed up both the desire of the industry to optimize its benefits under ACA and its fear of the alternative. The bill would, AHIP claimed, "destabilize the individual market; cut Medicaid; pull back on protections for pre-existing conditions; not end taxes on health insurance premiums and benefits; and potentially allow government-controlled, single-payer healthcare to grow" (quoted in Hellmann, 2017, para.1; see also Pear, 2017). The implication that Republicans' actions were driving towards a government-run healthcare system, of course, stands reality on its head, but also emphasizes the ferocity with which industry defends its expanded, government-subsidized coverage.

When these repeal attempts ultimately failed, Republican tactics shifted toward the elimination of the individual mandate. With escalating yearly tax fines, the mandate was intended to ensure that large enough beneficiary pools would make more tenable the extension of lower-cost plans that meet ACA coverage criteria. Defending the basis for the ACA's insurance exchanges, AHIP (with other groups) warned of "serious consequences if Congress simply repeals the mandate while leaving the insurance reforms in place: millions more will be uninsured or face higher premiums, challenging their ability to access the care they need" (America's Health Insurance Plans *et al.*, 2017). While insurance exchange markets had met with mixed success initially, by 2017 they were starting to meet their profit potential for industry (Abelson, 2017). With millions of new enrollees on the exchanges, their effect had become a palpable—albeit still a minority—component of industry profits. In the end, even the powerful healthcare lobby could not forestall Republicans' political urge to somehow make good on 9 years of very public ACA repeal pledges, and the individual mandate fell victim to the very instrument that gave it life—budget reconciliation. The exchanges, however, had taken root, and there has been only a modest drop in participation, with 11.5 million beneficiaries in 2020, even without any compulsive tax enforcement (The Kaiser Family Foundation, 2021).

Elsewhere, industry continued to struggle to preserve and optimize the general structure of healthcare delivery modeled by the ACA, even as the Trump administration and a Republican House had the law in its crosshairs. Industry lobbied aggressively to remove the Independent Payment Advisory Board, which theoretically controls payments from Medicare to purchasers and providers alike. They pushed back against a rule change proposed by the administration to allow small businesses to purchase "association plans," which offer far less protection than ACA-enforced plans (Demko and Cancryn, 2018). Similarly, the industry fought the "Cadillac tax," intended to raise revenue by taxing high-priced insurance plans. As a result of these efforts, the tax's implementation was twice delayed and then eventually repealed—along with the health insurance tax and the medical device tax—in late 2019 (Haberkorn, 2018; Keith, 2019). Ultimately, strategic maneuvering by industry has preserved spending levels mandated by the ACA while eliminating its revenue-raising elements—elements that were largely taken from industrial profits. At each turn, the imperative has been clear: maintain robust government involvement while maximizing profit streams.

Failing all else, Republicans turned to the courts (again), in *California v. Texas* (formerly *Texas v. Azar*), attempting to dismantle the ACA, by declaring it unconstitutional. Plaintiffs, who prevailed in District Court, argued that the entire law hinges on the sanctity of the individual mandate, which accorded it federal jurisdiction. With Republican tax reform having 'zeroed out' the individual mandate tax penalty, plaintiffs asserted that the ACA is unconstitutional in jurisdictional terms (Keith, 2018). Taken up by the Supreme Court in 2020, as the Trump administration expressed its unwillingness to defend the law, the insurance industry intervened as a 'friend of the court,' making clear that:

> Even assuming the Court has reservations about the constitutionality of the individual mandate and the severability of that provision from the ACA (either in its entirety or in part), the profound harm to the public interest flowing from either a grant of preliminary injunctive relief or a grant of declaratory relief—through detrimental impacts on patients, governments, health insurance providers, medical care providers, and other stakeholders —compels their denial (America's Health Insurance Plans, 2018, p. 7).

Similarly, the AHA insisted that "striking down the entire ACA would devastate this Nation's healthcare system, its patients, and the hospitals they rely on for care" (American Hospital Association, 2018, p. 3). For purchasers and providers alike, a return to healthcare delivery with no community rating or guaranteed issue rules in the purchase of health coverage, along with retraction of Medicaid and Medicare funding, would shrink the now government-bolstered marketplace in health, definitively raising premiums in an unequal manner. As such, with the exception of the National Federation of Independent Businesses (NFIB), which has opposed the ACA from the beginning, no sector in the health industry backed Republican designs on the program's dismantlement.

Ultimately, from its Medicare Advantage favourability, to expanded Medicaid in over 30 states, to a government-propped individual market open to price increases, the ACA has been a very productive terrain for the health industry. And while each industrial group within the sector cannot and does not retain fully optimized profitability in the face of the law's volatile political course, there has been a concerted effort across these groups to capitalize on government spending while minimizing both revenue contributions (such as taxes or industrial discounts) and market risk. The ACA is not so much government 'meddling', as its loudest critics suggest, but rather a government reassurance to many sectors benefitting from and seeking to expand market-oriented health in the US.

4.3 Conclusion: The Future of US Health

The overall picture of the US healthcare system can be described as a patchwork, with grossly uneven coverage across the population. Among those who profit handsomely from this arrangement, there is no serious appetite for change or simplification. Indeed, it is precisely the complexity and cumbersome nature of unlimited contracts in US health that makes it such a lucrative sphere of accumulation. But even if this complexity has typically achieved profits beyond expectation, like any sphere of accumulation, there are limits. In a market that expands on the basis of rapid price increases and enlarged care opportunities, political questions have been legitimately raised as to why some Americans receive so much healthcare and others so little, even none. This has also been the entry point for adaptive accumulation, at the crossroads between an industrial need for new profit outlets and the crisis of inadequate care generated in a fragmented market system of health delivery. From Medicare Advantage to ACA insurance exchanges, stabilized and expanded forms of industrial revenue have been procured while insurance, pharmaceutical, and hospital trade groups make moral and political arguments for the protection and well-being of US citizens/patients. In a sector where other comparable OECD states make the health industry bend to governmental and public purpose, a long history of reform has left the US government accommodating multi-pronged industrial interests, in order to extend expensive and objectively ineffective market-based care.

At writing, the ACA has persevered through the Trump administration and its contempt for 'Obamacare', even surviving the Supreme Court challenge in *California v. Texas* (Luthi, 2021). Moreover, 2020 – 21 has witnessed probably the worst US health crisis on record, with COVID-19 leading to the death of well over half a million of its citizens, a health system in disarray, and a politico-economic situation that has grossly divided the nation. It could be argued that healthcare, in particular, has reached a critical conjuncture and, more than any other policy area, is ripe for serious structural reform. In a telescoped manner, COVID demonstrated the harm done to impoverished and racialized communities in an unequal and uneven health and social system (Cox and Krutika, 2021). The disproportional and unequal impact of the virus has provoked another political debate around healthcare accessibility and equity, giving rise to new calls for some form of single-payer healthcare, best captured by the popular and political movement towards 'Medicare for All' (MfA).

The concept and initial legislative steps for MfA have been on the table since 2016, largely propelled to the national stage by Senator Bernie Sanders' two presidential campaigns. At first glance, the proposal is alarmingly simple. US Medicare, the largest single-payer health system in the world, possesses popular appeal, and the aim is to expand its domain to include larger portions of the population, with an eye, ultimately, to cutting out insurance companies from core healthcare provision. The benefits of this to the US population are undeniable—access to healthcare would increase while its costs would decline, largely as a function of massively broadened risk pools; lowered administrative costs; and public leverage over the upward march of provision costs. Indeed, the Congressional Budget Office has scored this program recently, estimating its current legislative form to lead to enhanced healthcare usage, but an overall drop in healthcare costs of $650 billion (Gaffney, Himmelstein and Woolhandler, 2021). On the issue of inequalities, revealed so clearly during the pandemic, universal and equitable healthcare access will not solve every social ill, but it will go some distance towards mitigating one of most trenchant social stress points across racial, gender, and class lines in America.

It has also become clear that this has some popular appeal across US political culture, at least when represented in general terms. In the wake of COVID, frequently conducted polling places support for a publicly-funded healthcare system above 70 percent (Michels, 2021). But as has often been the case with healthcare polling data, the devil is in the details. More detailed polling suggests that simply not enough people believe or understand that universal, single-payer healthcare would constitute a major change to the current system of delivery. Critically, more than half of polling respondents believe that such a system would not require them to relinquish their private plans, whether acquired via employment, through Medicare/Medicaid, or on ACA market exchanges (Altman, 2020). This inconsistency reflects overall confusion in a healthcare system that is unnecessarily but strategically complicated, and it forms the basis from which both industrial and political resistance to change will continue to emerge.

Political momentum towards Medicare for All has certainly built beyond previous expectations, with over a hundred Congressional Democrats signing on and a House hearing scheduled in 2021. However, arrangements under adaptive accumulation will not be relinquished without a colossal fight from the health industry, which has already organized aggressively. Indeed, following the Biden electoral victory in 2020, AHIP, in concert with Blue Cross-Blue Shield, immediately staked out its ground, issuing a letter to Congressional leaders. Getting ahead of calls for government run healthcare, it instead stressed the necessity of increased subsidies to both COBRA premiums (allowing people to keep private, employer-based plans after termination) and individual market premiums. At the same time, the letter demanded stabilization of funding to Medicare Advantage plans, with an extra emphasis on MpD (America's Health Insurance Plans and Blue Cross/Blue Shield, 2020). That AHIP uses the critical situation surrounding COVID to call for an expansion to all the component parts of its government adapted strategy should come as no great surprise. Tragically, crises are often simultaneously opportunities for capital. Equally unsurprising, but perhaps more disappointing, is the rather obedient response of Democrats. While Sanders' legislation lingers in the background, Democratic lawmakers, following Biden's lead, have moved ahead to inject billions into precisely the revenue streams sought by industry. The COVID Relief package passed by Democrats provided an additional $35 billion to increase subsidies for private insurance plans under the ACA and Cobra mechanisms. Record lobbying of the health industry —$615 million in 2020—makes this outcome all the more understandable (Evers-Hillstrom, 2021).

In this regard, the difficulty of the path to be forged ahead in American health delivery could not be more apparent. Industry, having pushed the limits of profit accumulation through MA, MpD, and the ACA, will forcefully advocate for a system in which the competitive market mechanisms within these programs are validated, while government subsidization expands progressively, always avoiding markets deemed of little value. In this, there is perfect consistency in the industrial call for *both* an expansion of the healthcare exchange markets *and* enhanced Medicaid funding. The latter cleans up the inevitable adverse selection in healthcare purchasing, allowing for unprofitable quarters of society to be sidestepped, without any sullying association to industry. In the end, of course, this is far more expensive for society. A recent study of private coverage *versus* Medicaid costs concluded that,

> ... overall healthcare spending was more than 80% higher among Marketplace-eligible adults than among Medicaid-eligible adults. This difference was no longer significant when claims were adjusted to Medicaid prices, indicating that the cost differences were driven by higher prices for the same services in the Marketplace compared with Medicaid (Allen *et al.*, 2021, p. 9).

Higher payments and overall societal cost equal enhanced profit in the marketplace, and no small amount of these costs are born by individual beneficiaries.

> Marketplace coverage was also associated with 10-fold higher out-of-pocket costs for low-income enrollees than Medicaid. This finding is consistent with prior research that found

that Marketplace enrollees are exposed to higher out-of-pocket costs and are at greater risk of extremely high spending even with significant federal subsidies (2021, p. 9).

Finally, defensive claims that market actors deliver higher quality care also found very little corroboration.

> In terms of clinical quality, we found no difference for the primary outcome of ambulatory care–sensitive hospitalizations. Among secondary outcomes, 5 measures favored Marketplace coverage (though 1 was of minimal clinical relevance, a 1 percentage-point difference in flu vaccination), 1 measure favored Medicaid, and the rest (6 of 12) showed no significant differences (2021, p. 9).

There can be no doubt that industry—from insurance to hospitals to pharmaceuticals—seeks to avoid instances of government-run programs (except for the extremely impoverished) that offer even a slight demonstration effect on costs to the American public. Medicare for All, of course, constitutes the worst of all outcomes for corporate actors, which is why the industry gears up so readily each time there is even the prospect of reform. The reasons for this are clear: single payer health insurance would lead to enhanced healthcare use but a significant drop in overall social spending. Industry wants no part of this, as its powerful fights against state-based public payer models in Michigan, Washington, Colorado, and California make abundantly clear (Michels, 2021; Rock, 2021; Wilkins, 2021).

Short of a universal payer model, even second- and third-best options draw fire from industry and its supporters. Dropping the eligibility age of Medicare to 60 or 55 would include more people on the public healthcare rolls, and it has been suggested that this could be done without Congressional approval through Executive Authority. What this would mean in terms of the private market is not clear, as such a large portion of Medicare is already operating outside the normal boundaries of traditional Medicare. Will new enrollees have access to Medicare Advantage or will they be limited to traditional Medicare? How would either differential access or complete reversion to TM be sold politically? Both of these questions offer obvious points of vulnerability and, thus, opportunity for AHIP, PhRMA, and the AHA to exploit during any politico-legislative process.

Similarly, the seemingly endless quest for a so-called public option is likely to fare no better. This was the target of AHIP, even as it espoused political support for the ACA, and it is unlikely to sit idly by while Congress ponders such an option (Strasser, 2012). Even if such an option were to emerge within ACA coverage, it would likely exhibit a weak systemic effect and could rather easily be discredited. A public option would not start out with very much (if any) purchasing leverage, assuming the healthcare law were rewritten to allow for robust price negotiation. If the vast majority of healthcare purchasing agents surrounding a public option are still market-oriented, that program is still likely to pay out market level prices. And there should be no illusions about the costs: serving marginalized and impoverished communities, the provision needs will be all that much greater. In the end, the public option, with a weak actuarial risk pool, and without any substantial single-payer price leverage, will appear costly and bloated. It will be low-hanging fruit for anti-government conservatives and the health industry, offering little more than a demonstration case as to why government should not be allowed to 'take away your healthcare choices'.

Ultimately, any realistic assessment of healthcare reform in the U.S. steers us towards an all-or-nothing conclusion. Either there is a sea-change in at least purchasing (a single-payer system), where either government(s) or highly regulated and coordinated non-profit associations take the helm, or adaptive accumulation will continue to rule the day. Corporate actors, along with policymakers of all stripes, have proven adept at creating a complicated labyrinth of purchasers and providers, where the possibilities for commercial intervention abounds. And once in place, the notion of selectively 'taking away' citizens' existing commercial healthcare plans, whatever their actual efficacy, has proven to be a political dead end.

Chapter 5: Education Reform and Adaptive Accumulation

If healthcare rivals the military domain as a component of total societal spending, then education is not far behind. Spending in K-12 education exceeds $600 billion across the U.S., and the wider education 'market', estimated at $1.3 trillion, has hardly gone unnoticed by the business community (Zion Market Research, 2018). As with health, citizens involved in the private education endeavors are captured participants, because opting out of the existent resources available to them is rarely a viable option. Parents need their children to attend school, and all too often this is not under conditions of their own choosing. The US educational landscape has been changing for some time, but unpacking this change in an understandable way can prove challenging, as funding and delivery are spread across federal, state and local jurisdictions.

This chapter undertakes this task by considering the degree to which education, like health, has become a robust terrain for adaptive accumulation. It asserts that, in fact, K-12 education is on a concerted transformative path to adaptive strategies, even if that process is nowhere near full realization. And, as with health, this transformation preys on the racial and class inequalities built into the American education system. The room for accumulative expansion is extensive, but this has also been tempered by the considerable political sensitivities attached to education reform. As such, reformers zero in on, or manufacture, 'crises' as a key motivator to change, whether such change is welcomed or not by the communities it affects.

The chapter opens with a brief background discussion of crisis-creation in early neoliberal approaches to education, which sets the stage for waves of reforms in the contemporary era. Following this, it delves into the field of reforms, from charter advocacy to private corporations, in order to reveal the extent of active restructuring. Private entrants into this market have evolved over time, and adaptive accumulation, it turns out, can progress amidst a range of both profit and non-profit actors. The chapter goes on to examine the role of government in partnering with such actors, fostering a regime increasingly conducive to the private consumption of public revenues. Finally, it turns to the nagging problem of evidence, which critics of public education insist predominantly favours increased market involvement. While much of this favourable 'evidence' amounts to anecdotal stories, these are magnified in ways that heroize market options, equating them inherently with individualized success. Ultimately, however, this anecdotal projection belies the facts, as any *systematic* study reveals widespread underfunding of public education and no improvement (and often deterioration) with the increasing participation of market actors.

5.1 Education as Crisis

It has been well established that neoliberalism, from its outset, puts pressure on the credibility of the state as a manager of societal affairs. This, however, is not a pressure that could be applied without rhetorical justification, and the primary way to substantiate it has been to proclaim 'crisis'. Probably nowhere has this strategy been more relevant than in the field of education. In the late 1970s, the precursors to Reaganomics were in full swing, and the formation of groups like the Business Roundtable put the forces of the market at the center of societal transformation. Such groups set their sights on education as an arena ripe for reform. Antonia Darder (2015) has pointed out that, in retrospect, this was consistent with the motivations of neoliberal reformers:

> It is not surprising that just as promising outcomes in the late 1970s and early 80s with improvement in educational outcomes for the most impoverished communities and an increase in college and university attendance by historically underrepresented student populations, the conservative antics of the right revived their bitter campaign to discredit progressive educational efforts, advance the privatization movement and usher in some of the most Draconian accountability measures in the history of US education (2015, p. xi).

It is important not to romanticize the postwar gains of African-American communities, or the degree to which their court-affirmed civil rights—especially in education—were actually realized in the post-war era. But there is no doubt that some educational gains had emerged for these communities, and from the perspective of the political right, these were perceived as encroaching on their own standing. In line with the wider neoliberal distaste for any Keynesian structures, public education, then, would become emblematic of all that needed to be dismantled or held at bay.

It was the Reagan administration that cleared the ground for this by deploying its most damning political thematic: the economic 'failures' of the welfare state. According to the administration's landmark report, *A Nation at Risk*, the downward trend of American economic prowess could be traced to the failing state of public schools. It asserted that, "the foundations of our society are presently being eroded by a rising tide of mediocrity that threatens our very future as a nation and a people" (quoted in Slater, 2015, p. 4). Students experiencing debilitating distractions (primarily drugs), failing teachers, and a general inability of public institutions to address societal ills are said to have combined in a critical mass, necessitating new ideas in educational reform. Graham Slater (2015) has noted that this agenda found acceptance across business circles and the mass media, with a constant portrayal of public education as an economic obstacle in the path forward. He notes that mass media "propagated the script of public education as the source of every social ill from the failure of big business to compete globally, to the loss of jobs, to a rise of youth murder" (2015, p. 5).

A primary outcome in education policy under Reagan was to shift its emphasis from the impact of social inequalities to the purported impacts of teacher and student performance. Educational improvement was sought at the local school level, with teacher quality review, student testing and parental choice. Pedagogical outcomes were evaluated at the level of the individual, understood to be is entirely responsible for both his/her circumstances and results. This, then, became the insertion point for 'accountability' as a quantified form of school evaluation (through test scores and performance metrics) and, ultimately, the basis for parental 'choice' in school selection. The political fights around school vouchers and charter schools find their roots in this policy shift, and educational institutions, like all government-related bodies, went from being the object of federal support to targets of shame and ridicule.

While the first Bush administration focused little on education policy, it carried forward the main outlines of this vision with increased standardized testing. But as with so many policy areas, it was the Clinton administration that pushed forward market friendly measures in ways unimagined by previous Republicans. With what Richard Van Heertum and Carlos Alberto Torres (2012) call 'instrumental progressivism', the administration integrated the fundamental principles of Republican educational reform, wrapped in the guise of a new knowledge economy. While the administration dropped the crisis rhetoric, the underlying motivation of its policy remained the same: achieving global competitiveness, this time in a 'knowledge economy'. Rather than moralizing, the administration sought to gift the troubled American worker with enhanced knowledge, and students were to be the beneficiaries of the future. As such, the education agenda during this period advocated standardized testing, teacher quality programs, expansion of Head Start, lifelong learning, and the proliferation charter schools (2012, pp. 10 – 11).

From Reagan to the end of the Clinton years, we witness the reimagining of public schooling, such that it better reflects entrenched neoliberal values. The foundation for more prolific changes in the 21st century is set during this period, including the imperatives of individual student autonomy and flexibility, teaching scrutiny, and the right to school choice. Education is a sensitive societal issue, not easily amenable to change, and neoliberal philosophy was, arguably, applied in a hesitant and haphazard manner. Other than generalized rhetoric against bureaucratic inertia, with alternative schooling experimentation, its strategies did not yet meet with a wider economic strategy on the part of corporate actors. However, with a new Bush administration at the outset of the millennium, as well as a new 'crisis', education would proceed from a Republican and Democratic centrist hobbyhorse to a sphere of considerable interest in the corporate world.

5.2 Mining Public Schools

If the corporate response to reforms in education policy were tepid during the 1980s and 90s, that changed definitively at the turn of the century. The enormous sums of public revenue flowing into primary and secondary education make it a very attractive target for private operators. As one investment advocate has made clear, "[even] in the most trying economic times, hundreds of billions of taxpayer dollars, earmarked for the education of children ... are appropriated each year. For ... private equity and venture capital firms, that kind of money can prove irresistible" (Herbert, 2014, para.15). As a public domain, K-12 education is attractive to strategies of adaptive accumulation, because there is no question of the consumption of the commodity. It is not a luxury but a necessity and, as such, consumption cannot be suspended in periods of slow growth. In this sense, education is quantitatively and qualitatively ideal. It is a sphere in which both new markets can be established and unusually stable profit streams emerge, as funding from public revenue sources become more or less guaranteed.

Private K-12 education has existed in conjunction with the public system for a long time, but the emergence of charter schools opened a doorway for capital *into* public schooling. As suggested above, charters emerged in the 1990s as the preeminent form of 'alternative' schooling. With an emergent perception of 'failing schools', particularly in the urban environment, charters began as a community-driven attempt to revitalize local education. These schools remain part of the public system, supported by public funds, but they are reconstituted under a charter that grants them autonomy from local school board, municipal, and state authority. This allows discretionary freedom on budgets, and it also accords autonomy in hiring and firing, circumventing teachers' unions. While charters grew haphazardly in the 1990s, their numbers have grown rather dramatically since the turn of the century. In 2000, there were some 1900 charter schools, but this number had far exceeded 7000 by 2018, providing schooling for well over 3 million students (National Center for Education Statistics, 2018). Meanwhile, the number of students attending public schools between 2005 and

2016 actually dropped by over half a million. These figures vary across different states quite substantially, but a number of states have seen charter schools climb above 10 percent of student population, including Florida, Louisiana, Arizona, Utah, Colorado, Michigan, Delaware and the D.C. area, where the figure is over 40 percent (National Center for Education Statistics, 2019). What is the significance of these inroads? While all charters are not private, *per se*, their autonomy and decentralization of authority opens multilayered possibilities for corporate insertion, where the utilization of public funds can be adapted in ways that enhance private returns and evade public accountability.

From the early 2000s, the rush was on to realize for-profit schooling in as many locales as possible. Charters became the order of the day, as strategies around flipping such institutions into business or business-like entities emerged. The procedure is fairly consistent: locate districts with so-called failing schools, encourage their conversion to public charters, and wait for their need for management. A charter school that has been delinked from the district board is more vulnerable to investment and management by private operators (Saltman, 2014, p. 241). The main vehicle for doing this has been the educational management organization (EMO), which typically operates a network of schools, often across regions. EMOs can work on for-profit or non-profit basis, though their goals often appear strikingly similar, as the latter are regularly allied closely with the business model. Almost half of all EMOs run on an explicit for-profit model, and they can administer dozens of schools across state boundaries. It is increasingly the case that these organizations negotiate agreements with schools rather than district boards, suggesting that the charterization process itself has become a major mechanism for the re-routing of education revenues into private channels.

EMOs are now able to legally operate in over 35 states, and they manage almost half of all charter schools. The concentration of these management arrangements is very clearly urban and disproportionately aimed at poor and racialized communities. There are, of course, multiple avenues by which EMO/Charter arrangements can render private benefits, but it starts with the awarding of public funds to the schools themselves. These revenues are primarily local, but can also be sourced from state and federal sources. Charter schools negotiate contracts with EMOs to oversee the daily operational delivery of education and asset management. The school's board then largely becomes a financial clearing apparatus, with only broad decisions on how to use funds being transferred over to the EMO. The point should be clear: as revenues move further and further away from the public sector, the accountability of their use diminishes. As Bruce Baker and Gary Miron (2015) have made clear, the transparency of EMOs—for-profit and non-profit—is far weaker than a public institution. Non-profits are largely shielded from statutory accountability, with the only remaining assessment being the spotty requirement that IRS filings be disclosed. In for-profit EMOs, transparency amounts to either Securities and Exchange Commission quarterly reports, in the case of a publicly traded company, or nothing at all.

This lack of transparency has consequences, as funds are utilized in questionable and highly varying ways. The assumption that a non-profit EMO is more inclined to use public funds in an appropriate and pedagogically productive manner does not bear out. In the case of both for-profit and non-profits, there is opacity in the use of funds and a clear predilection towards cost-cutting. As with all publicly derived revenues, usually the stipulated amount is fixed, in this case on per-student enrolment basis. As such, the route to either profit accumulation or enhanced utilization of revenues (in the case of a non-profit) is cost-reduction. And here, the rule of business is clear: money spent on students does not go towards the financial health (bottom line) of the organization.

Charter schools under contract, then, tend to be resource poor, in relation to both physical assets and operational costs. Textbooks, materials, cafeterias, extra-curricular equipment, and student support all suffer in this environment. As one educator described it in Chicago, at the epicenter of Charter school conversion, "[as] soon as I went inside, I could see that it was built on the cheap. There was no gym; students just had to go outside throughout the winter. There was no lunchroom. Instead, tables were set up in a hallway, and lunches were brought in from outside the school" (Rawls, 2013, para.18). Above all, of course, it is personnel—the most expensive budget item—that is most vulnerable to cost reduction, and teaching instruction and remuneration is being decidedly reduced (Howley and Howley, 2015, p. 31). Yet, managerial overhead, particularly in contracted management corporations, continues to climb at an unhealthy rate. Six-figure salaries are the norm, where CEOs of school networks can make 250 percent of the salary of the Superintendent of the New York City School System, while administering a fraction of the student numbers. Such salaries occur under the murky category of 'administrative expenses', which remains unelaborated as a budget item, but is twice as high in EMOs than either district or school boards (Baker and Miron, 2015, p. 26).

The administration of network schools involves, increasingly, a diminished and, ultimately, Taylorist form of education. This begins with standardization, and the move to bring curriculum under the regime of student testing and performance score evaluations. This systematically ignores cultural, social and political barriers thrown up against individuals, groups and classes, and it marginalizes particularly low-income and racialized communities. Indeed, despite "the increasing gap between the ultra-rich and the rest, the U.S. believes it is a classless society and will not acknowledge these broader issues in the classroom—it's easier to provide a test score and then blame teachers and the kids for failing" (Spreen and Stark, 2014, p. 156). The goal is to introduce standardized testing and, especially, test-preparation materials, making the quantitative comparative examination of results easier. This data-driven form of educational practice has led to the growth of supplemental education services, whereby large publishing companies, such as Pearson, Houghten Mills and Princeton Review, as well as a range of new firms, can provide myriad preparation, testing materials, and data services to a growing number of public and non-public schools. Additionally, the pressure to perform has opened up the supplemental tutoring industry, where companies such as Sylvan and Kaplan offer additional tutoring services, often subsidized by public funds (2014, p. 160). As we will see below, this metrics-driven pedagogy is advanced by both the state and representatives of corporate America, with burgeoning multi-billion-dollar industries as the prime beneficiaries and questionable results for parents and students.

The standardization of materials, however, positions companies as far more than just 'suppliers' of material. Instead, they are the architects in devising *how* teaching materials are arranged, along with their accompanying objectives. These firms often serve entire networks (whole districts or multi-district 'markets'), and their reach in terms of educational content is extensive. The discernible element of adaptive accumulation is unmistakable: firms are becoming decisively more influential when it comes to actual decision-making in education. There is no process more central to public policy in education than curriculum development, and this is exactly the nature of the work being taken up by numerous contracted and sub-contracted companies.

> From one perspective, these activities simply represent efforts by districts to leverage the resources and infrastructure of the private sector in order to meet accountability demands. However, taken together, they add up to something much more that has important implications for firms' relationships with districts. When school districts purchase products and services from firms such as SchoolNet, they are in essence hiring private firms to act as critical extensions of educational central policy processes—to set preferences for what educational outcomes matter, to track educational outcomes, and to design interventions based on these outcomes (Bulkley and Burch, 2011, p. 241).

Firms carry the veneer of public status, as they seek out ways in which schools can excel at standardized learning, or they utilize data management to determine which schools are falling short. And they do so in confusing ways, wherein it may appear that multiple companies are involved in different elements, such as test creation, after-school programs or tutoring. Often, however, these are subsidiaries of the same firm, involved in a package delivery of services, known as a 'wrap around' (2011, p. 241). More insidiously, standardization becomes increasingly the yardstick for the wider public school system, as governments seek to expand existing contracts with corporations already involved in charter management (Spreen and Stark, 2014, p. 160). As firms reach into an estimated $80 billion market in ancillary services, they increasingly absorb substantive responsibilities appropriately reserved for the public domain

With the routinizing of pedagogical materials, an important element—mentioned above—of service delivery remains: teaching labour. Teaching is the most cost-intensive element of any school, and the degree to which professional remuneration and benefits can be minimized has substantial impact on the bottom line of EMOs. In this, the charter school movement, with management organizations leading the charge, have been highly effective in reducing labour costs, resulting in the diversion of revenues elsewhere. As mentioned, charter schools have a far greater degree of autonomy over hiring and firing practices, and they generally are able to operate outside of the union framework. With this, their practices zero in on the utilization of teaching staff that is substantially less experienced, resulting in far lower salaries than district public schools. According to Baker and Miron (2015), "[it] is becoming increasingly clear that low cost labor, in the form of young, short term teachers, is a feature and not a bug of the business model of many charter school EMOs. Staff turnover—diminished employment longevity—also serves to reduce long term health costs and retirement benefits costs" (2015, p. 23). The authors have confirmed this pattern for non-profit and for-profit EMOs alike. For instance, in two of the largest non-profit networks, KIPP and Harmony schools, the utilization of younger, more inexperienced staff (1–5 years teaching) is maintained by aggressive yearly turnover, and they suggest, along with others, that this trend is reproduced at a national level. In fact, in a critical study on teacher turnover rates, researchers found that teachers are twice as likely to leave charter schools as traditional schools, correlated to a variety of factors, including minimal teaching experience; weak or no teaching certification; part-time teaching status; and, especially, much lower union membership (Stuit and Smith, 2012, pp. 273–274).

This supply of younger, cheaper, and more flexible labour has not been procured spontaneously. Fitting into the broader neoliberal move in education, external organizations, such as Teach For America (TFA) and New Leaders for New Schools, have developed alternative teacher training programs designed for labour flexibility and low cost delivery. These programs aim to provide certification for teachers outside of a university degree framework. The training is much shorter, and the programs are not state accredited.

> TFA leads the nation in the quest to create alternative teacher certifications; it supports the dismantling and restructuring of public schools in urban communities; it provides a con-

stant supply of new TFA recruits to replace fired teachers at urban schools; and it actively participates in the creation of new charter schools or alternative neoliberal educational projects (Baltodano, 2017, p. 151).

The aim of charter networks, particularly in urban areas, is to utilize short-term teaching labour and promote a network of alumni, aiming for a 'rationalized' management of schools. All too often, this involves a hard line with student performance, eviscerating the personal, racial, familial, community, and/or politico-economic context of students as underlying causes of their underachievement.

TFA has been enormously successful in spreading the charter model, and its personnel have reached the highest level of network management. Undoubtedly, the most famous is Michelle Rhee, who has been called the 'face of the corporate reform movement'. Rhee became Chancellor of the Washington, DC school system, with only 3 years of experience in the New Teachers Project in Chicago. With no experience of public administration, and a deep mistrust of its officials, Rhee devastated the public school system, firing over half of the teaching staff and a third of the school principals (2017, p. 151). The aim, of course, was to replace these personnel with alternatively certified teachers, graduates of TFA and other institutions, and extend a business model of school administration and pedagogy. This included an augmentation of funding from philanthropic sources (more below) to establish "school choice, merit pay for teachers in exchange for the eradication of tenure, and the use of private providers to run schools" (Scott, 2009, p. 107). Such models are standardized across for-profit and non-profit networks centered in urban environments, such as Chicago, Philadelphia, Los Angeles, New York, New Orleans, and Detroit.

Teaching labour, it turns out, is not the only object of strategic behavior on the part of charter schools and management organizations. Students, too, can be 'farmed' in ways that optimize school performance, generating more positive statistics and, ultimately, securing or boosting revenues. In healthcare, this is known as 'cream skimming', whereby the healthiest patients are granted insurance and, with this, overall beneficiary payouts for healthcare coverage are reduced. In example after example, it has become clear that charter schools, under the direction of network management, are pulling higher-income, advantaged students from public systems. This is measured through the percentage of students receiving free or reduced-price lunch, and charter enrolment repeatedly yields a demographic profoundly altered from the surrounding pubic district (Burris and Bryant, 2019, p. 16).

Practices and policies that discourage enrollment, deny enrollment or drive students out of charter schools not only fly in the face of the whole notion of 'choice' (whose choice is it, then?) but also work to increasingly segregate the most vulnerable or disadvantaged students in traditional public school systems while siphoning off much-needed resources that support them. Discriminatory enrollment practices are widespread, having been documented in multiple states (2019, p. 18).

Additionally, most district revenue models apportion school budgets on a per student basis, with additional amounts for students with disabilities and/or learning challenges. The statutory responsibility of charter schools to receive such student populations vary by state, but there is clear evidence that management networks approach these situations strategically. Depending on the law, schools either avoid serving such students or carefully choose which disabilities they will service (Baker and Miron, 2015, p. 19). In this way, statutory requirements are met, also boosting revenue, but the more progressive cases, requiring more personnel and resources, are avoided.

Before teachers or students can even enter the school, however, new structures of accumulation can be put in place, primarily in real estate, building, and lease arrangements. What can only be described as real estate 'schemes' have proliferated around the Charter and EMO model, operating legally but surely pushing the boundaries of ethical behaviour. Schools are not typically understood to be real estate investments, but since the spread of management models, they have become just that. The schemes involved are usually quite complex, involve considerable conflict of interest, and they often hoist double payment obligations on public revenue sources. As such, even in the most optimal cases,

... the policies designed to enable the acquisition and transfer of major capital assets result in the losses of resources that might otherwise be spent in classrooms. In worse cases, they result in substantial losses and diversion of resources, often difficult to evaluate due to the complexity of financial transactions and relationships among various parties (2015, p. 27).

Across the charter school movement, there is a need for capital assets (i.e. land and buildings), but the charter's utilization of tax revenues is statutorily prohibited from involving capital investments and long-term debt. Normally, such investments in the public system are undertaken through municipal bonds, rated highly, with low interest rates, given the guaranteed basis for repayment. Charter schools, in association with management organizations, therefore, must find alternative routes to securing assets. They do this in two ways, but always with a third party, either of their own creation, as with a non-profit financing entity, or mingling with outside investors, usually a real estate investment trust (REIT). In the case of the former, a revenue bond is raised by the third-party entity, in order to finance the purchase of assets (usually formerly public schools), on the presumption that it can lease the building to the school, and its rental payments (backed by public funds) will cover the bond. As a lower rated bond, the interest payments are higher, and this greater amount of revenue diversion drains resources away from the school's budget. The more aggressive for-profit approach is REIT, which involves shareholders who extend capital investment to the trust to make a property acquisition. The trust, in turn, leases the property to the charter and then collects on a 'triple net' lease; wherein the lessee pays monthly rent, taxes, insurance, and maintenance costs. These substantially larger lease payments are utilized to pay any debt obligations, after which at least 90 percent of taxable earnings must legally be distributed to shareholders (2015, pp. 28–42). It should be no wonder, then, that school investments have grown into one of the 'hot' real estate investments, pulling in major financial actors, such as PNC Financial, Prudential, US Bank and Goldman Sachs (Rimbach and Koloff, 2019).

Three major problems exist in this arrangement. The first is the extraordinary drain on public resources, which should be going towards the education of students. These resources are instead accumulating in bondholders' and shareholders' investment portfolios. The second is the extraordinary nature of deals that sell off public assets, without voter consent, and then force public taxpayers to pay the mortgage on now private holdings for public use. Public revenues are, thus, paid out twice for the same property and, in the end, the public holds no equity. Finally, the 'arm's length' relationship between school board officials, financing entities, EMO officials, REITs and shareholders is often highly circumspect. The prevalence of self-dealing and conflict of interest in these transactions has become increasingly clear, and it is in no way limited to particular states or districts (Strauss, 2020).

In everything from test preparation to physical buildings, private agents are transforming public revenues into avenues of profit. And it should be clear that the designation of 'non-profit' in no way signals a more anodyne version of this process. In fact, non-profit status can bring egregious violations of public trust. Certainly, when IDEA Public Schools, a non-profit charter school network, attempted to lease a private jet for almost $2 million per annum for its board members, such excess was on full display (Strauss, 2020). The endless array of examples beyond this singular executive largesse should signal the degree to which K-12 education has become a boon for investors. Moreover, "regardless of their for-profit or nonprofit status, the majority of charter schools bring in substantial salaries to their administrators and profits to their contractors" (Spreen and Stark, 2014, p. 167). It is, however, critical to note the enduring public status bestowed upon these same actors (charter schools are public if receiving public revenues), affording them extraordinary political cover but also decisive policy roles. This should be understood as more than a set of processes in which school districts merely utilize outside contracts. Rather, when viewed as a complete ensemble of agreements, there is a blending of public and private purpose here, in which "districts are in essence hiring private firms to act as critical extensions of educationally central policy processes—to set preferences for what educational outcomes matter, to track educational outcomes, and to design interventions based on these outcomes" (Bulkley and Burch, 2011, p. 241).

This staple of adaptive accumulation—a public persona among private actors—would not be possible without the necessary ideological and material undergirding that accompanies capitalist social relations. A critical ally in this regard has come in the form of philanthropic organizations, led by prominent capitalists in US society. These figures have collectively come to be known as 'edupreneurs' for their willingness to wade deeply—both philosophically and financially—into the terrain of K-12 education. They articulate their own pointed views on educational policy in the U.S., usually a pronouncement of 'failure', and they back such assertions up with funding across a variety of organizations that are willing to support their message. In this sense, they are markedly different from conventional philanthropic organizations, such as Carnegie or Ford Foundations. Conventional philanthropies advocated broadly for change and the public good, even if this was bounded ideologically. They issue support to *existing* efforts by inviting applications in broad areas of public concern. But the terrain in foundational funding for K-12 education is different, captured by the terms 'venture philanthropy' and/or 'philanthrocapitalism'. While these terms have often been utilized interchangeably, and while they certainly contain overlapping objectives, they are not, strictly speaking the same kind of organization.

Venture philanthropy involves a series of prominent non-profit organizations, aggressively focused on market-oriented social objectives. In its differences with past foundations,

> venture philanthropy treats schooling as a private consumable service and promotes business remedies, reforms, and assumptions with regard to public schooling. Some of the most significant projects involve promoting charter schools to inject market competition and 'choice' into the public sector as well as using cash bonuses for teacher pay and to 'incentivize' students (Saltman, 2009, p. 54).

Familiar names—almost synonymous with American capitalism—play an outsized role here: the Gates, Broad, and Walton Foundations are among the biggest players. The Gates Foundation has poured millions into programs aimed at shutting down 'failed' public schools and supplanting them with school choice. It has been particularly active, along with the Broad Foundation, in supporting the Knowledge Is Power Program (KIPP) network of schools; has injected $100 million into New York City school restructuring; sought urban reform across the country; and supported multiple management organizations (Baltodano, 2017, p. 149). For its part, the Broad Foundation's support of KIPP has been in keeping with its top-down understanding of educational reform, as that series of schools has become infamous for its disciplinarian teaching approach. Moreover, it has issued the Broad Prize for Urban Education, introducing a funding model that compels resource poor urban schools to compete with each other (2017, p. 148). Rounding out this list, the Walton Foundation has been advocating and supporting enhanced 'school choice' (read: charter expansion) since the late 1980s. These are, of course, not blind donations, and venture philanthropists require a return on their investment. This is measured in student performance rates, expansion of EMOs and Charter schools, and "the growth of constituencies who will place political support on public officials to support particular educational reforms" (Scott, 2009, pp. 116–117).

The advent of philanthrocapitalism is, arguably, more deleterious. It involves the establishment of organizations which are for-profit and, therefore, not subject to the same reporting rules. This means that billionaires, such as Mark Zuckerberg, can purport to donate large portions of their wealth, directed at ostensibly public and benevolent purposes. In reality, Zuckerberg's founding of CZI, a so-called for-profit philanthropy, points to some of the more blatant methods of adaptive accumulation utilized in the sphere of education. CZI is a limited liability corporation (LLC), and it is privately owned, with no public reporting requirements. Its main objectives are to advance personalized, pay-for-service educational programs and to enhance mass student data accumulation for downstream market uses, primarily in targeted advertising (Saltman, 2018). Zuckerberg claims to have donated the equivalent of $45 billion to CZI, but there is absolutely no way to know whether that is true, or how the organization utilizes the funds it does have. Indeed, philanthrocapitalism "represents an effort to collapse the distinction between public and private spheres and between profit seeking and charity" (2018, p. 61). In this grey zone between charitable largesse and business, philanthrocapitalists have the capacity to disrupt education policy—as Zuckerberg did in New Jersey—while expanding profit opportunities.

In both the non-profit and for-profit versions, private foundational support is critical to the growth of the charter movement and management networks, as it generates overlapping and reinforcing funding sources for advocates while also dovetailing with targeted governmental programs. Given the wide socio-cultural absorption of neoliberal values, the words of Bill Gates carry as much weight (possibly more) than the Secretary of Education: "Our high schools are obsolete.

By obsolete, I don't just mean they're broken, flawed or under-funded .... What I mean is that ... even when they work exactly as designed, our high schools cannot teach our kids what they need to know" (quoted in Saltman, 2014, p. 256). This denunciation has been echoed by other philanthropic organizations, and they advocate relentlessly for an accelerated pace of change in school reform. With targeted, multi-year funding, they are able to catalyze reform—very often in poor urban areas—in an accentuated manner. Beyond this, however, they provide the ideological barrage necessary to help school choice, business management models, and increased standardization take hold throughout the country. In fact, they insert themselves across a wide but selectively targeted set of institutions, funding "a range of organizations including advocacy organizations and think tanks, university-based researchers and research centers, individual schools, and advocacy organizations" (Scott, 2009, p. 114). Combined with their already outsized political influence, the socio-political fabric in which corporate philanthropic actors operate is being transformed, where the utilization of public dollars to bolster a business model in education is, quite simply, being increasingly normalized.

The corporate encroachment on K-12 education has been pronounced, and there is every reason to expect its continuing expansion. In its explicitly for-profit or various non-profit guises, the openings for material (and ideological) gain remain unbounded. Corporate actors, new and old, grapple onto this manifestation of adaptive accumulation, because public revenues remain far from exhausted, and these actors have proven adept in their ability to transform these revenues. From a business standpoint, the 'future' is here in K-12 education, and the future looks good.

5.3 Governmental Market Makers

The deft maneuverability of corporate actors would not be possible without an amenable governmental apparatus at their disposal. Education in the U.S. operates primarily at a state, municipal and district level, but the federal government has become increasingly involved, utilizing a carrot and stick approach to incentivize the direction of policy and reform. Indeed, federal administrations have done a considerable amount to expand charter schools across the country, and this has proven to be a bipartisan effort.

While Republicans have exhibited an outright hostility towards the Department of Education since its inception under the Carter administration, it was the second Bush administration that expanded the department's influence substantially. Seen through the lens of adaptive accumulation, Republican distaste for either governmental intervention or largesse is expressed by redirecting resources into market actors' hands rather than eliminating them. In this case, the administration's early signature legislative achievement—No Child Left Behind (NCLB)—has become almost a cultural touchstone in relation to federal education policy. Famous for its pre-school and early reading programs, NCLB is much more than this, ushering in a new era of school restructuring and reform. Bush had instigated such changes as Governor of Texas, and his administration sought to ramp these efforts up to a national level achievement.

The legislation focuses clearly on standardization methods, using test scores as the measure for school success (Cohen and Lizotte, 2015, p. 4). In doing so, it advances performance-based outcomes for schools, measured in so-called annual yearly progress (AYP). Over the course of the administration, this brought about two major outcomes. The first involved the mandate for schools at the primary and secondary level to improve their outcomes on a yearly basis. The criteria are, perhaps not surprisingly, unforgiving, as schools are not afforded the overall increase in funding that would help to generate such improvements. Instead, the legislation requires that schools grant access to secondary educational services, redirecting existing public funds. This is, of course, "a boon for testing and tutoring while it doesn't provide financial resources for the test scores it demands" (Saltman, 2007, p. 134). The effect has been a normalization of outside contracting across school districts that would not otherwise have engaged in such practices. On one level, this has meant the utilization of outside services to create benchmarks of accountability, such as online platforms that project accountable data regarding school and student performance. But in addition to this, schools *must* make available outside instruction—*via* companies such as Sylvan and Kaplan—to bolster their AYP outcomes. NCLB, then, has almost certainly stimulated "the demand and supply of educations services and products in the market place by reducing financial risks for companies and not-for-profits," and, more importantly, "enhancing the perceived legitimacy of private engagement in public education as a reform strategy" (Bulkley and Burch, 2011, p. 244).

A second and more pernicious outcome of AYP standards relates to its underlying political objectives. With upward creeping performance indicators, NCLB very quickly became a vehicle with which to identify so-called failing schools, and then a closure mechanism for districts, as the federal government threatened to revoke funding. The reach of these standards spreads surprisingly far: in 2010 – 11, it was estimated that 48 percent of all schools would not meet AYP (Spreen and Stark, 2014, p. 164). Writing on the insidious manner in which school systems from Chicago to New Orleans have been leveraged by AYP measures, Kenneth Saltman (2007) suggests that,

NCLB is setting up for failure ... public schools nationally by raising test-oriented thresholds without raising investment and commitment. NCLB itself appears to be a system designed to result in the declaration of wide-scale failure of public schooling to justify privatization. Dedicated administrators, teachers, students, and schools are not receiving much-needed resources along with public investments in public services and employment in the communities where those schools are situated. What they are getting instead are threats (2007, p. 136).

There is no doubt that the bulk of 'failures' are being identified and acted upon in dense urban, low-income areas. These are zones in which political agency among community members is diminished, and the prospect for redirection of public funds into the hands of private actors meets with less resistance. In this way, federal policy dovetails particularly with municipal policy, oriented as it is around planning for district and community 'rejuvenation'.

In fact, it is this municipal connection that forms the arc through which the Obama administration, for all its fanfare around 'change', intensified the connection between federal policy and corporate-friendly reform. The appointment of Arne Duncan, former CEO of Chicago Public Schools, was a critical link in this chain. Duncan oversaw the Chicago Renaissance 2010 program, which sought extensive closure of 'failing' public schools and an expansion of the charter system across the city. Set up by the Commercial Club of Chicago, the program targeted 15 percent of Chicago schools to be closed and replaced with 100 Charter (or otherwise experimental) schools, often located in gentrifying areas of the city. The array of reformed schools varied in character, depending on the neighbourhood in which they would be situated. Affluent areas, or areas seeking affluent in-migration, were accorded superior academic programs, with hand-picked administrators and teachers (as well as students). Besides feeding directly into the pernicious speculative urban real estate market, this emboldened the ongoing reality of student and teacher segregation (Jankov and Caref, 2017). Poor communities, on the other hand, "were forced to grapple with their neighborhood schools being gutted and transformed into test-polluted, overcrowded and debilitating commercial institutions" (Carr and Porfilio, 2011, p. 8). Moreover, Duncan was on the leading edge in creating military style academies, advocating the value of both military discipline for student development and recruitment programs.

It is this legacy that blossomed in the Obama administration, with the full embrace of school reform. At the time, this met with considerable consternation among even those who placed hope in the new administration.

It is difficult to understand how Barak Obama can reconcile his vision of change with Duncan's history of supporting a corporate school reform and penchant for zero-tolerance policies .... At the heart of Duncan's vision of school reform is a corporatized model of education that cancels out democratic impulses and practices of civil society by either devaluing or absorbing them within the logical of the market or the prison (Giroux and Saltman, 2009, p. 776).

In the first year of its mandate, the administration put in place the Race to the Top (R2T) program as the centerpiece of its education policy. The program, promulgated as part of the American Reinvestment and Recovery Act of 2009, allocated $4.35 billion to a competitive program, in which states could contend for funding based on particular criteria. In effect, these criteria validated the objectives of NCLB, and created a strong continuity between the Obama and Bush administrations on K-12 education policy. In order to receive funding, states had to demonstrate success along four separate criteria, including "adopting rigorous standards, recruiting and retaining effective teachers, turning around chronically low-performing schools, and building data systems to track student achievement and teacher effectiveness" (Bulkley and Burch, 2011, p. 244). With competitive funds in play, R2T set in train a process of accelerated school reform and charterization, as states introduced charter schooling into their system or expanded existing caps on such institutions.

Having set off a flurry of activity around charter schooling, standardization and performance evaluation as a means to access federal funding at the state level, R2T also dovetailed with philanthropic goals. Indeed, the program utilized competitive grants to encourage the adoption of standardization, including the Common Core State Standards (CCSS) developed by the National Governors' Association, but funded in its design and promulgation by the Gates Foundation. The story of CCSS is a remarkable one of philanthropic intervention and rapid nationwide uptake of an educational program. R2T is not responsible for CCSS, *per se*, but its stipulation that states put in place 'college and career ready' standards to gain access to competitive funding amounted to all but a structural endorsement of the standards (Layton, 2014). According to a one-time federal education policy architect, turned critic,

> [the] federal government, states and school districts have spent billions of dollars to phase in the standards, to prepare students to take the tests and to buy the technology needed to administer them online. There is nothing to show for it. The Race to the Top demoralized teachers, caused teacher shortages and led to the defunding of the arts and other subjects that were not tested. Those billions would have been better spent to reduce class sizes, especially in struggling schools, to restore arts and physical education classes, to rebuild physically crumbling schools, and to provide universal early childhood education (Ravitch, 2016, para 8).

This would, eventually, be finalized in the promulgation of the Every Student Succeeds Act of 2015, albeit with slightly modified relationships between federal funding and standardization. The act, which updates and replaces NCLB, still calls for standardized testing, but its execution and implication falls more squarely with state agencies to determine. State agencies have long since set their sights on combining federal and philanthropic funding as means to bolster state education budgets, which, in turn, ensures that both charter reform and standardized evaluation are here to stay (Charest, 2017).

Indeed, it is hard to imagine that the federal government would be willing to shift direction on educational reform, when the overall trajectory of its funding base is increasingly tied to this dual dynamic. And private providers know full well that, once ensconced within such a critical area of public policy, their removal from service delivery presents an intractable political liability. There are, of course, nominally successful charter schools (more on this below), most of them in wealthy suburban or semi-suburban areas. Reversing course will require a large-scale reinvestment in publicly accountable educational facilities, raising the ire of those in the community with the most political clout. As such, in addition to ideological commitments to market-inspired delivery, the rolling forward of programs in the face of deeply problematic outcomes has continued, on the basis of political pragmatism.

On a programmatic level, the charter phenomenon displays institutional dysfunction and questionable personnel behavior that would be damning for any public agency. This has been exemplified most recently in a detailed study of funds utilization in the national Charter Schools Program (CSP). CSP was put in place in 1994, and received an injection by the Obama administration to the tune of $4.5 billion, with an eye towards both expanding successful existing programs and providing funds for the creation of new charter schools. The report, issued by the Network for Public Education (NPE), amounts to a damning review of CSP's fiscal accountability and deeply troubling institutional outcomes (Burris and Bryant, 2019). By the reviewers' estimations, the program's disbursed funds amount to over $4 billion, and from this, over a third of all funded schools either did not open or opened and closed quickly thereafter. This has totalled over a $1 billion in evaporated public funds, for which there exists little to no accountability. The report, which has received national and Congressional attention, suggests a deep lack of accountability standards, insufficient monitoring, and outright fraud. It rolls out a rather overwhelming set of cases, demonstrating the deeply problematic use and abuse of federal public revenues. Among the numerous criticisms of the CSP presented in the report, the authors point to the many grantee institutions enacting barriers to enrolment aimed at higher cost students, primarily those with disabilities; blatant conflicts of interest between the various elements of charter education delivery; and the declining quality of grant applications as the program has proceeded (2019, pp. 2–3).

Somewhat more alarming is that fact that the Department of Education (DOE), through the disbursement of these and other funds, has clearly ignored the findings of its own internal reviews. The DOE's own Office of the Inspector General (OIG) issued reports in 2016, 2018, and 2019 that reflect the same dynamics examined in the NPE report. These reports are highly critical of the department's failure to monitor or evaluate its own disbursement of funds. They point, specifically, to 1) the widespread dangers of financial risk, including waste, fraud and abuse; 2) lack of accountability, including conflict of interest and inappropriate spending authority; and 3) performance risk, with inappropriate procedures and spending irregularities among management organizations severely jeopardizing learning requirements (US Department of Education, Office of the Inspector General, 2016, p. 16). The 2018 report makes clear that across the various funding sources in the department—well beyond but also including CSP—there was a failure to monitor state education agencies (SEAs) in relation to school closures. In the three significant states reviewed, Arizona, Louisiana, and California:

> The SEAs generally had procedures and controls to identify the causes for charter school closures and for mitigating the risks of future charter school closures. However, the SEAs did not always meet the Federal and State requirements when (1) performing close-out procedures for Federal funds a charter school received, (2) disposing of assets a charter school acquired with Federal funds, and (3) protecting and maintaining student information and records from closed charter schools. For 46 of the 89 charter schools we reviewed, we found that the SEA and/or authorizer did not ensure that Federal funds were properly closed out within 90 days of the school closure as required by Federal laws and regulations. The SEA and/or authorizer also did not ensure that assets acquired with Federal funds were properly disposed for 65 of the 89 charter schools. In addition, for 39 of the 89 charter schools, the SEA and/or authorizer did not ensure that student information and records were protected (US Department of Education, Office of the Inspector General, 2018, p. 8).

Ultimately, in all of these matters, "the Department did not provide adequate guidance to SEAs on how to effectively manage charter school closures. In addition, the Department did not monitor SEAs to ensure that [they] had an adequate internal control system for the closure of charter schools" (2018, p. 8). This broader review of federal spending and state oversight, in the wake of previous critical reports, signals a structural aversion to viewing charter school reform with any critical detachment, assuming instead that local officials would proceed with best practice.

Even as the Department's OIG undertook an in-depth review of a single educational management organization, the response appears to have been muted. In 2019, the office investigated Individuals Dedicated to Excellence and Achievement (IDEA) Public Schools, an EMO that services some 44,000 students across

Texas and Louisiana(US Department of Education, Office of the Inspector General, 2019). From 2014 through 2018, IDEA received $108 million in replication and expansion grants from the federal government, some $39 million of which had already been spent by the time of the report. The findings of the OIG, however, did not suggest that this $39 million had been tracked for its impact over time. In fact, the overwhelming majority (61 out of 74, or 84 percent) of performance measures required by the DOE had not been reported. IDEA did not supply guidelines to its staff for recording these requirements, nor did it demonstrate that it had in place a process for recording such data, were they to be collected. Moreover, spending of grants exhibited irregularities, including unallowable expenses and inadequately documented expenses (2019, p. 2). This detailed review of one management organization points to a pattern of inadequate regulatory terrain, identified and exploited by a corporate agent, in order to access extra revenue *via* non-repayable federal grant money. While a competitive environment for funds has certainly been created at the federal level, the manner in which recipient programs claim 'success' remains opaque, because regulatory officials, on the whole, seem disinclined to interrogate or monitor such claims in a meaningful way.

This barrage of criticism concerning weak regulatory structure paralleled the election of the Trump administration and the confirmation of his Secretary of Education, Betsy DeVos. While the administration signaled a turning point in an array of public policy areas, K-12 education cannot really be said to be one of them. DeVos had been a long-time reformer in the state of Michigan, the state furthest down the path of charter reform in the country. And like Arne Duncan, this history exhibited a less-than-glorious trail of reforms, in which public revenues were diverted into a glut of charter schools that propped up an industry but failed to have any meaningful positive effect on Michigan K-12 students. A recent exposé made clear that,

> Michigan's K-12 system is among the weakest in the country and getting worse. In little more than a decade, Michigan has gone from being a fairly average state in elementary reading and math achievement to the bottom 10 states. ... Indeed, new national assessment data suggest Michigan is witnessing systemic decline across the K-12 spectrum (Binelli, 2017, para.21).

It has become abundantly clear, even among initial proponents, that charterization in Michigan has less to do with quality of education and more to do with the corporate capacity to compete for public revenues (an annual $7600 per pupil in Michigan), such that resulting management contracts are profitable for EMOs, financing organizations and other contracted parties.

In this sense, the DOE did not take a particularly different tact with DeVos at its helm, but instead forged ahead with Obama-era charterization, regardless of the results. DeVos had to answer to Congress for the damning NPE report, but her answers were not especially elucidating. She insisted that the report was 'propaganda' and 'riddled' with errors, despite the fact that when asked to produce failure rates of charter schools, she could produce no such data (Ujifusa, 2020). More telling is the fact that although DeVos proposed a cut of $5.6 billion from the department's budget, she advanced an increase to charter school grants, with the CSP dispersing $65 million in 13 grants going exclusively to large EMOs. These included a number of organizations caught up in various spending and political scandals, such as IDEA schools, which came under fire for keeping a $2 million luxury jet and $400,000 in tickets and a luxury box at San Antonio's AT&T Center (Greene, 2020). While ideological devotion to market-based choice may have been more blatant with DeVos, the overall trajectory of charterization and the highly permissible terrain granted by the federal government remained largely the same. DeVos, like her predecessors in the Obama and Bush administration, progressively expanded the field in which EMOs and charters operate, opening up new revenues for private actors across the education field. And in spite of evidence in terms of educational outcomes, highlighted below, this expansion continues to find popular political resonance and has no shortage of advocates.

5.4 Education and the Culture of Choice

Amidst the seemingly relentless drive towards school 'choice' and 'reform', it behooves us to ask: has it worked? Has the creation and ongoing expansion of the charter industry—for profit and non-profit alike—led to a discernible improvement among US students? Even if we stick to the standardized criteria set out by charter proponents, the answer, by available data, is a resounding no. A Stanford study from the Center for Research on Education Outcomes demonstrated results across 16 states that were less than promising, to say the least. When evaluated alongside comparable public schools, the study found modest growth in student learning in 17 percent of charter schools; no improvement in 46 percent; and 37 percent of such students did worse than their public counterparts (Bulkley, 2011, p. 114). The DOE's own study on student achievement in charter schools hardly came to more inspiring conclusions: in terms of academic performance, "on average, study charter schools did not have a statistically significant impact on student achievement" (Gleason *et al.*, 2010, pp. 6–7). Moreover, the study looked at 35 other outcomes, including absences, suspensions, and indications of student effort, well-being, behavior and attitudes, and parental involvement, and found "no evidence that study in charter schools had any impact on the majority of these outcomes" (2010, pp. 6 – 7). For all the political energy exerted over the benefits of 'choice' in education, the evidence for charter success is, at best, limited to anecdotes. Indeed, the most positive conclusion that can be drawn from the data above is that billions spent on educational reform has not, *on average*, worsened an already bad situation for American students.

Such a conclusion, however, amounts to little more than an abstract statistical indicator, obscuring the concrete situation of students, particularly in poor, urban locales. The impacts on cities such as New York, New Orleans, Philadelphia or Detroit (to mention a few) are not suggestive of increased access and equity for those who need it most. In Chicago, for instance, the racial impact of education reform has been pronounced:

> In Chicago, high-stakes testing, top-down accountability, the aggressive expansion of charter schools, the use of test scores to label and brand "failing" schools, mass closures and consolidations of neighborhood schools concentrated on the predominantly Black South and West sides of the city, investment and growth of selective enrollment schools, have all occurred without displacing the entrenched segregation of CPS. Instead, corporate education reforms have worked to reinforce segregation as an institutional pillar of the opportunity structure in Chicago, even as it has transformed the particular manners by which segregation and educational opportunity relate (Jankov and Caref, 2017, p. 24).

The picture repeats itself from urban zone to urban zone, wherein closures disproportionately affect minority students, who are then shuffled off to insufficiently resourced schools. As Saltman (2014) points out, 'failure' is "selectively deployed, and is racially and class coded" (2014, p. 255). The unstable status of these reforms—through fraud, mismanagement, closure, etc.—means that there is no guarantee that students will complete their studies there. And this attrition dynamic grossly skews measures of success in charter schools, as low-performing schools are regularly purged from performance measurement—an option not so readily available in the traditional public setting. Along the way, it is especially poor minority communities that bear the brunt of this damage.

It is worth recapping the element of adaptive accumulation that taps into social resentment and wider neoliberal, anti-government sentiment. Adaptive accumulation is neither synonymous with racial animus nor its direct cause—racism has a long trajectory in the United States that cannot be reduced to class. But this form of accumulation does harness existing racial and class dynamics in ways that afford new and unique avenues of profitability. Race-targeted school reform, whether highlighted or not, becomes both the repository for blame (underperforming communities) and redemption (choice, 'what works', innovation). In this sense, adaptive accumulation utilizes existing American societal resentment, infused as it is with racial bias and communal segregation. From within resource poor communities, competition, shame, anxiety, anger, and aspiration are all sentiments that can provoke demands for change, with an eye to market fulfillment. From outside such communities, racism, resentment, indifference, and impatience inform a 'corrective' approach to ongoing educational restructuring that, more often than not, results in a disciplinarian rather than empathetic approach. When such sentiments receive the blessing of public revenues, the spaces for direct and derivative accumulation open up.

In this way, the adaptive accumulation strategy of reform advocates—particularly industry—taps into both the disciplinarian and aspirational elements of racialized community settings. On the disciplinarian side, educational reform directs social anger at both students and teachers, faulting them for failure in already grossly under resourced and under serviced communities. Students are individualized in a manner that subjects them to the rugged demands performance measurement. Often this occurs in ways that involve strong punitive techniques. 'No excuses' and zero-tolerance policies, as well as actual militarized education settings, have become a widespread element of charter schooling among marginalized populations. The Broad Foundation, for instance, has fostered this in large-scale charter projects, such as KIPP:

> KIPP schools have been accused of harsh, punitive policies, and violations of state and federal laws. One such example is the campus at Fresno, California where students complained about teachers and administrators humiliating and isolating students for misbehaving (forcing a student to sit and bark like a dog), removing their eyeglasses and other personal belongings, withholding recess or lunch, and implementing social isolation policies to ostracize those students who dare to challenge the KIPP rigid compliance model ...(Baltodano, 2017, p. 148).

This strict pedagogical tactic has come under criticism for its discriminatory element. One widely cited national report investigated a broad array of charter schools across the country, finding that black and Hispanic students are disproportionately punished, including suspension (a dangerous trend, as it is seen as a gateway to 'dropout' status). More alarmingly, and regrettably aligned to corporate procedures elaborated above, students with disabilities were suspended at 235 schools at a rate of 50 percent or greater (Losen *et al.*, 2016). The notion that pre-emptive disciplinary tactics can usher individual students along a 'corrective' path carries a deeply individualistic, retributive component, reminiscent of a highly flawed American criminal justice system. As some critics have pointed out, "... more and more schools are breaking down the space between education and juvenile delinquency, substituting penal pedagogies for critical learning and replacing school culture that fosters a discourse of possibility with a culture of fear and social control" (Giroux and Saltman, 2009, p. 773).

Simultaneously, the punitive ethos constructed around student discipline and performance is accentuated in relation to teachers. In the popular domain, public school teachers have become the unwilling symbols of a perceived bloated and ineffective government bureaucracy. On the one hand, this has translated into a disastrous material handling of the profession, with "sweeping rollbacks in work security, mandated dissolution of unions, and new forms of invasive (and misguided) scrutiny" (Sturges, 2015, p. 8). The effects, particularly in areas heavily influenced by charter reform, have been pronounced, with droves of teachers either being dismissed or leaving the profession voluntarily. This could not happen, however, without an enabling cultural environment, which has been handily shaped across the charter managerial movement. Media studies conducted on the discursive handling of traditional public teachers *versus* 'certified' TFA teachers present a very clear trend. Veteran teachers are seen as intransigent, bureaucratic, resistant to pedagogical innovation, while certified teachers are seen to outperform, to "bring something to the table, or as a 'pipeline of talent'" (Gautreaux, 2015, p. 8). Teaching, long a poorly remunerated, unforgiving career path, is being shaped into a repository for communal and parental anger, undergirding demands for reform.

This directed blame may instigate a new 'common sense' among students, parents, and communities, but adaptive accumulation also requires a sense of political agency related to market-oriented activity. In this sense, there is no denying that charter schooling has garnered advocates, even in impoverished and marginalized communities. Herein lies the aspirational element of educational reform, wrapped up in the discourse of 'choice'. Advocates have zeroed in on parents' frustration with chronic underfunding, community abandonment, and high dropout rates, suggesting that the real problem is bureaucratic inertia, and the solution is putting student placement under the authority of parents. Market reform, here, becomes the common-sense action, empowering communities to change the structure and outcomes of the educational system, with the parent-citizen as its heroic protagonist. In this discursive-ideological move,

> ... what the charter school movement accomplishes politically is to conflate the opportunity to *choose* education alternatives with the agency to *produce* these alternatives. In other words, market-based school reformers tend to gloss over the disparities in access to the means of production of school alternatives even as they tout charter schools as providing a level playing field in which parents can make rational choices to maximize their children's opportunities (Cohen and Lizotte, 2015, p. 1830).

This classic confusion of equality of choice with equality of outcome is presented by advocates in the language of civil rights. Reformers suggest that they are merely standing up for the rights of the downtrodden, leveling the playing field for victims of racism and/or poverty. So-called parent trigger laws, which allow for parents to petition for low performing schools to convert to charter or be taken over by an EMO, are a decisive part of this process (Scott, 2011). The publication of films, such as *Waiting for Superman* or *The Cartel*, strongly reinforce this message of parental 'revolt' in the name of equality, waged against oppressive bureaucracy and corrupt teachers' unions. Even in relation to "their potential to create equality of opportunity, however, they fall short. This is because market reforms are disconnected from other forms of social inequality and fail to adequately provide for equal access to high-quality, well-resourced, and diverse schools" (2011, p. 586).

Ultimately, there is no call to equality in the wider social or even policy environment—only the right to access charter or private education, supported by public funds. The sense of urgency and clearly defined targets of reform advocates—boards of education, administrators, teachers—fits well into the political culture of resentment and disciplinary redemption. In this sense, adaptive accumulation across the educational sphere operates within a complex terrain of political struggle, wherein proponents find cultural acceptance even among those who least benefit from reform.

5.5 Conclusion

Education has been a sphere of public policy that, at least until the 2000s, remained largely unscathed from the neoliberal assault on all things Keynesian. This is not to say that education flourished in the United States, as poor urban and racialized communities have been starved of vital resources for many decades. But since the embrace of 'school failure' during the second Bush administration, a more contemporary political economy has taken over, whereby 'failure' is utilized as an inroad to private revenues. As with healthcare, this does not involve a wholesale retrenchment of the state, or even its hollowing out. Critics of reform have made clear the difficulty in elucidating this process analytically, because terms such as *privatization* do not really capture its essence. As its enhanced involvement suggests, from federal funding, to Title I regulations, to SEAs, we find a robust governmental presence. Ultimately, this involves harnessing and/or adapting state structures, from school boards to Congress, in order to devolve regulatory governance and budgetary management onto a competitive field of private organizations.

As particular urban zones are flooded with competitive players, as has occurred in Michigan, California, Texas or New York, the continuing significance of government funding is readily apparent. Stepped up government funding and charter expansion, as well as their directed collaboration with venture philanthropists and philanthrocapitalists, constitutes the fuel that drives this competitive terrain. Adaptive accumulation results from corporate players—from large managerial organizations to small resource-centered niche companies—seeking to expand the public budgetary portion that is directed towards this growing sector. As this proceeds, it is important to consider "... not only the impact of *individual* actors on children and schools but the broader effects of private engagement on the overall provision of publicly funded education ... [and] public purpose" (Bulkley and Burch, 2011, p. 248). If the costs of such accumulation are diminished equity, waning democratic participation, and the instrumentalization of K-12 curriculum, there is a particularly discouraging environment evolving out of this unfortunate historical dynamic.

Chapter 6: Incarceration, Detention, and Adaptive Accumulation

Among the range of publicly organized functions in which private actors have realized profitable gains, probably none is more controversial than incarceration. While the overall budget numbers are not as high as healthcare or education, the political and cultural impact of decades-long swollen prison populations is unmistakable. Perhaps no other issue of adaptive accumulation captures more fully the contradictions and dilemmas of American political culture. Structural oppression, racism, xenophobia, individual responsibility, rights discourse, societal revenge, and anti-government mentalities all coalesce in public policy questions around incarceration.

Additionally, privately-based incarceration was one of the first arenas to provoke 'industrial complex' terminology outside of the military context (Donziger, 1996; Schlosser, 1998). And while there are long-standing historical cases in which private actors undertook incarceration on behalf of the state, the dramatic upswing of private industry's involvement coincides closely with increasingly neoliberal policy since the 1980s. This chapter addresses the manner in which market actors have utilized conservative trends towards 'law and order' policies, as a means to carve out profitable domains of accumulation. As in the cases of healthcare and education, it points out that the goal is not to displace government involvement. Indeed, the success of this industry is intricately bound up in governmental presence—tighter enforcement, harsher punishment, expanded incarceration facilities. Private actors seek a quasi-public role in augmenting select parts of this process—the profitable parts—while leaving the heavier consequences of mass incarceration to public authorities.

To advance this case, the chapter begins with a discussion of rising 'law and order' and 'tough on crime' policies in 1980s and 1990s. Punitive and racist policy dispositions are not caused by adaptive accumulation, but they are almost certainly the environment in which private actors recognized profitable opportunities. Following this, the chapter turns to a discussion of industry strategies within this sector, emphasizing actors' adaptive behaviours, as they have scrambled, successfully, to adjust to an on-again-off-again political environment around incarceration policies. Government, too, has adapted, and the third section highlights the willingness of policymakers at the federal, state and local level to pursue public goals through private channels. Importantly, this is not a uniform phenomenon, as policymakers act on highly divergent motivations, from the well-intentioned all the way to the deeply problematic. Finally, the social and political features of prison policy do not emerge without wider societal

https://doi.org/10.1515/9783110761801-006

participation, and the last section considers the complicated political culture in which this particularly sensitive arena of accumulation has arisen.

6.1 The Neo-conservative Turn and 'Law and Order'

As the Reagan administration brought extensive change in military spending, social policy, and the overall role of government spending, so too did 'law and order' policies enter a period a dramatic transformation. There is a prevailing notion that private incarceration and its perverse incentives have driven the incarceration rates of the US prison population. For instance, Karina Moreno and Byron Eugene Price (2018) emphasize,

> ... the fact that the War on Drugs and the tough on crime movement were facilitated by the powerful private prison industrial complex. Meaning, the industry that scored the lucrative and coveted government contracts to incarcerate felons *created* those felons through lobbying for harsher criminal justice laws and longer mandatory minimum sentencing laws, which they sponsored and drafted. Through millions of lobbying dollars donated to political parties, the private prison industrial complex was able to write the laws that resulted in an influx of prisoners, amassing unprecedented levels of profits (2018, p. 145).

While the private industry did eventually facilitate a harsher criminal justice system, it is inaccurate to position it as the cause. Rather, the expansion and intensification of law and order policies was, first and foremost, a highly racialized outcome of shifting politico-economic winds and cultural rhetoric from the 1980s onward, long before private incarceration corporations came forcefully onto the scene.

On a historical front, we can continuously backdate the origins of law and order policies, for instance, originating them in the Johnson administration's war on crime or Nixon's war on drugs. But like so much of the domestic policy stemming from the Nixon administration, its rhetoric never matched the actual policy outcomes. Instead, it is the dramatic shifts ushered in by the Reagan administration that signaled decisive change. The emergence of the new right at the end of the 1970s always meant more than the determined advancement of Chicago School economics, symbolized by figures such as Friedrich von Hayek or Milton Friedman. It was the coupling of market prioritization with social conservativism that ushered in the broad cultural appeal of the Reagan revolution and everything that followed. And social conservativism left a definitive mark in matters of criminal justice, as the administration used legislation and the institutional legacy of Nixon (such as the creation of the Drug Enforcement Agency, or DEA) to step up measures that would address perceived increases in criminal behaviour.

Here, it is important to note that the invocation of law and order policies by the Republican right were always both a determined political strategy and racially coded. The evolution from Barry Goldwater's heated language to Nixon's 'southern strategy' constituted a recognition that the grievances of southern white voters could be harnessed and allied to the party's traditional industry friendly constituency, creating an umbrella large enough to challenge the Democrats' general dominance in federal politics. Thus, the Nixon/Agnew transformation of the Republican strategy sought to utilize white resentment in the wake of the civil rights movement, along with denouncing the liberal elite and student radicals, in order to drum up fear of crime, drug use and 'undeserving' government redistribution. The dominant discourse surrounding the black community was effectively shifted, wherein the virtuous (white) middle class of America now required protecting from racially coded images of drug users, criminals and welfare freeloaders (Olson, 2008).

The Reagan administration took this up in concrete terms, pronouncing its own 'war on drugs' in 1982. By 1984, the Sentencing Reform Act was passed, wiping out federal parole, and the 1986 Anti-Drug Abuse Act went much further, utilizing mandatory minimum sentencing and supplying grants to states which did the same (Eisen, 2019, p. 32). With stepped-up conviction rates, so called 'Truth in Sentencing' laws became the order of the day for politicians seeking to brandish their law and order credentials. This occurred at the federal level but was taken up with aplomb at the state level, where the majority of criminal justice proceedings and incarceration occurs. Demanding that prisoners fulfil a stipulated majority of their sentences (usually 85 per cent), these laws spread quickly, with 20 states having such legislation by 1994. And while this may have been motivated by the Republican right, it proved bipartisan in character very quickly. Democrats were eager to show themselves as not 'soft on crime', evidenced most forcefully by the Clinton administration and the 1994 Crime Bill. This legislation incentivized prison building and truth-in-sentencing at the state level, and its effects were prolific. The cultural rush to punish was further accentuated at the state level by repeat offender laws, commonly known as 'three strikes' laws, invoking mandatory life sentences upon third offenses.

Moreover, according to Avlana Eisenberg (2016), the nature of parole itself came to change, contributing heavily to the growing incarceration trend.

> While parole and probation were once imagined as providing an alternative, community-based forum for transitioning back to society, and only parole violators perceived as dangerous would be returned to prison, increasingly, offenders found in violation of adminis-

trative procedures were returned to prison. In fact, the rate of incarceration due to parole violations and revocation—what some scholars refer to as "back-end sentencing"—has grown even faster than rates of incarceration over the last four decades. By 2007, the United States annually sent more people to prison for parole violations than it sent to prison for all reasons combined in 1980. Thus, the high rates of mass incarceration are not merely the result of new crimes; they also result from parolees returning to prison (2016, pp. 82–83).

This rush by elected officials to demonstrate their law and order *bona fides* led to dramatic increases in the prison population, far out of sync with other countries or previous periods in American history. Between 1973 and 2002, the incarcerated US population grew from roughly 200,000 to well over 2 million, representing a rate increase from 100 to 750 per 100,000 citizens (2016, p. 81). At its peak in 2009, there were over 2.4 million prisoners in the US, when federal, state, local and county jails are considered. Indeed, it has been poignantly noted that there are more prison and incarceration facilities in the US than there are degree-granting colleges and universities (Ingraham, 2015). Recent political and judicial developments at the federal level have brought about a population decline in federal and state prisons, amounting to approximately 11 percent between 2009 and 2019 (Carson, 2020). However, the overall level of incarceration was never limited to federal and state prisons, and accounting especially for local jails and immigration, incarceration remains staggering in the U.S. A far more accurate picture reveals a criminal justice system that "holds almost 2.3 million people in 1,833 state prisons, 110 federal prisons, 1,772 juvenile correctional facilities, 3,134 local jails, 218 immigration detention facilities, and 80 Indian Country jails as well as in military prisons, civil commitment centers, state psychiatric hospitals, and prisons in the U.S. territories" (Wagner and Sawyer, 2020, para.2).

The complexity of this prison population, as well as the much broader population affected by incarceration, cannot be understated. It is critical to emphasise the deeply racialized, gendered, and classed nature of this system. Black Americans make up 13 percent of the US population, but they account for 40 percent of those incarcerated. Women, too, are incarcerated at an accelerated rate, and have been for decades. In both cases, one overriding predictor holds true: poverty is deeply related to incarceration. The vast majority of those incarcerated come from impoverished circumstances, often incarcerated because bail is beyond their own means, or the means of those related to them (Looney and Turner, 2018). And cycles of reincarceration are hardly surprising, as poverty "... is not only a predictor of incarceration; it is also frequently the outcome, as a criminal record and time spent in prison destroys wealth, creates debt, and decimates job opportunities" (Wagner and Sawyer, 2020, para.31). We will return to the social and political culture that enables such bleak realities in the American carceral landscape in the final section of this chapter. Suffice it to say here that in the midst of this pronounced inequality, corporate actors have derived advantageous accumulation strategies. While it is not, as suggested, a terrain of their own creation, it has grown into a highly extractive one in which multiple and evolving avenues for profit arise.

6.2 Corporate Strategies in Incarceration and Detainment

Within this expanded incarceration landscape, corporate actors have carved out so-called niche activities, with an eye to extensive and relatively secure profits. As suggested, a more recent volatile political backdrop has made these profits somewhat less secure than first thought, and this has required deft maneuver in relation to public decision making. Overall, there is no doubt that incarceration remains primarily a public undertaking, with a budget of around $81 billion if spending calculations are restricted to prisons, jails, parole, and probation. This figure, however, does not capture all of the potential revenues circulating within this sector, as it excludes a range of indirect costs, the payment streams for which can be tapped by private actors. In a more far reaching estimate, the Prison Policy Initiative has included such costs as policing, judicial and legal costs (criminal not civil), asset forfeitures, bail fees, and costs to families (commissary costs, telephone costs). The figure, by their reckoning, reaches closer to $182 billion and supplies a more realistic evaluation of this sector's real revenue terrain (Wagner and Rabuy, 2017).

While not a serious rival to military, healthcare, or education spending, budget figures in the billions still represent an enticing terrain for corporate players. In 1984, as Reagan's war on drugs was getting into full swing, and state prison populations began to swell, the Corrections Corporation of America (CCA), now CoreCivic, opened its first private prison in Tennessee (White, Pena and Weiler, 2020, p. 103). At the time, public expenditures on incarceration amounted to $10 billion, a figure that would rapidly swell over the next 15 years. By 1997, there were 91 such facilities, and this has grown to some 190 prison and detention centers (Eisen, 2019, p. 42). There were always two major players in this industry, Core Civic and GEO Group (formerly Wackenhut), with a few other subordinate players, including Management and Training Corporation (MTC). Core Civic and GEO currently bring in revenues of $4.5 billion, from a total private market that exceeds $5 billion. These are substantial revenues for any corporation, even if their control extends to a definitive minority of federal and state facilities, somewhere between 8 and 9 percent of the total incarcerated population.

Adaptive accumulation in this sphere, in the first instance, requires the securing of contracts for facilities, existent or planned. Private corporations aggressively pursue contract possibilities at a federal and state level, seeking to provide facilities for local, state, and federal populations, but also the transfer of existing prisoners between state locales. This began in Tennessee and progressed steadily, with corporate players offering facilities at a *per diem* rate, and promising more efficacious and higher quality service than what public facilities could offer. Along the way, growth in private prison construction considerably outpaced that of public construction. As Lauren-Brooke Eisen (2019) has noted,

> ... prison construction took off in the late 1980s and continued growing until the late 2000s .... [Between] 1995 and 2000, there were more than 150 new private prisons built across the country compared to about 50 public prisons. And between 2000 and 2005, this trend continued with only two new public prisons constructed versus 151 private correctional facilities, which drove almost all of the increase in the number of prisons built (2019, p. 77).

The capacity of these corporations to turn a profit depends—at a micro level—on the same production strategy as all fixed volume contracts: cost control. As in healthcare and educational production, publicly tendered contracts demand successful management of projected service usage, and the difference between set government payments (on a per prisoner basis) and internally controlled incarceration costs determines profit levels. As such, the primary determinants of 'success' are both the volume of prisoners (more prisoners equal more revenue) and the stringent management of workforce, resources, and services.

In this regard, keeping these facilities growing in one way or another has been critical since the outset of the industry. The goal has been to ensure that those prisons which are to be built will reach capacity, or at least near capacity. Contracts are strategically directed at states or regions in which prison overcrowding is a major issue, such as Texas or California. In the latter, a 2011 Supreme Court ruling mandated that overcrowding issues be addressed, based on the Bill of Rights, offering a potential windfall for the industry, which had the capacity to rapidly absorb prisoner populations. This problem is hardly new, and with overcrowding as a recurring problem over the last three decades, prison corporations have positioned themselves as the private 'solution' to both this public policy dilemma and strained public finances. *Per diem* rates on prisoners offer stable revenue streams when sufficient volumes are guaranteed, and this is precisely what corporate actors build into their state and federal contracts. As in other cases of adaptive accumulation, corporate 'risk' in publicly tendered contracts is highly mitigated: guaranteed occupancy rates (and payment) inhabit some two-thirds of federal and state contracts, regardless of actual occupancy (In the Public Interest, 2013). These usually place the occupancy floor at 90 percent or higher. In this environment, corporations have regularly built prisons 'on spec', with an eye to filling them later, often with out-of-state prisoners from fiscally squeezed jurisdictions unable to handle rising inmate populations. Along these lines, prisoners undoubtedly have become tendered commodities, and guaranteeing their numbers constitutes an instrumental avenue of profit for the industry.

On a political level, as well, the industry has not been particularly shy about drumming up business. It engages in robust lobbying and influence efforts, wherein it both protects a generally industry-friendly policy environment and pursues beneficial specificities in the law and in policy execution. In the last 10 years, the industry's main players have contributed roughly $38 million to lobbying and campaign finance, operating at the federal and, especially, state levels (Center for Responsive Ethics, no date). These funds are targeted at individual campaigns that have the greatest effect on the industry, a fact which explains the surge in contributions through both the Bush and Trump administrations. Overwhelmingly, but not exclusively, these contributions are directed at Republican recipients, with a general objective of avoiding market adverse criminal justice reform. GEO, for instance, has made clear in its SEC filings that,

> ... the demand for our correctional and detention facilities and services, electronic monitoring services, community-based re-entry services and monitoring and supervision services could be adversely affected by changes in existing criminal or immigration laws, crime rates in jurisdictions in which we operate, the relaxation of criminal or immigration enforcement efforts, leniency in conviction, sentencing or deportation practices, and the decriminalization of certain activities that are currently proscribed by criminal laws or the loosening of immigration laws (US Securities and Exchange Commission, 2012, p. 30).

Efforts are also directed at specific policies of states, which could have beneficial effects on industrial outcomes. Core Civic professed anxiety to its shareholders in 2015 that "[legislation] has been proposed in numerous jurisdictions that could lower minimum sentences for some non-violent crimes and make more inmates eligible for early release based on good behavior" (Cohen, 2015, para.4). But the industry is interested in more than just tough law and order policies—it also actively pursues policies that carve out new niche areas of accumulation. In Arizona and Georgia, its lobbyists helped draft and pass legislation on immigration that was highly amenable to detention profits, and in Oklahoma they lobbied to increase misdemeanors to felonies, enhancing sentencing time and *per diem* revenues (Eisenberg, 2016, p. 107). These are but a slice of the many efforts to maneuver corporate interests within a publicly defined field, blending corporate objectives with public interest around law and order.

Once contracts are secured and politically protected, however, the cost of service delivery forms the basis from which these corporations draw their profit. And it is here where the fundamental split with public purpose is most apparent. Corporate players maintain that they will offer the same services as public institutions, arguing that their advantage lies in the qualitative equivalence of their incarceration methods combined with a capacity for cost-saving innovations. The claims of CoreCivic (then CCA) make this clear.

> [We] have redefined the way prison facilities operate, combining cost-efficient procedures and modern security technologies. In fact, in the last 15 years, CCA has revolutionized the corrections industry ... We have to win every contract by proving we can build, operate, and/or maintain a facility more efficiently and more effectively, without compromising public safety (reproduced in Burkhardt, 2019a, p. 207).

This tends, quite frankly, not to be the case, as the entire business model depends on lowering costs of delivery. These reductions are especially focused on labour, which amounts to the majority of operating costs in incarceration facilities. The key, not surprisingly, is to tap into non-union labour forces, which require a lower pay rate and, importantly, considerably less training. On average, the average pay rate for private prison correctional officers is some $7000 per annum less than in the public sector—a gap that has grown over the last 20 years (Eisen, 2019, pp. 27–31). Training is substantially reduced for private sector guards, and job turnover is substantially higher, ensuring that a higher proportion of guards are working at entry level wages. A 2004 study demonstrated a turnover rate of 42 percent in private facilities, compared with just 15 percent in the public sector (Blakely, 2004, p. 29). High turnover rates, of course, suggest job dissatisfaction or anxiety in a complex occupational environment, where work experience and training matters.

> Compare the correctional officer's routine of checking cells for contraband, monitoring inmate movement, and ensuring doors are locked against the subtler and perhaps more important skills of handling inmate grievances, disciplining inmates, as well as helping them through family and other personal crises. It is easy to see how the former can be reengineered for less skilled, lower paid workers. It is more difficult to see how the latter skills can be simplified using a cookbook approach (Gaes, 2019, p. 285).

Routinization of labour skills in the prison environment moves incarceration further away from a rehabilitative effort towards a more blatant housing-storage-lockup endeavour. The general results of this are not encouraging, as a Department of Justice, Office of the Inspector General (OIG) report made clear. The OIG's criticism was multi-pronged, finding that private prisons were correlated with an increase in incidents *per capita* (in 6 out of 8 categories); safety and security deficiencies; and improper (far too frequent) use of special housing units (SHUs), commonly understood as solitary confinement (US Department of Justice, Office of the Inspector General, 2016).

None of this is to suggest these institutions are entirely bereft of quality control mechanisms—they cannot lay claim to public funds and provide a completely hollow service. It is, however, reasonable to assert that they do not accomplish the market-related claims of even their most moderate advocates. There is simply no substantial evidence that demonstrates either enhanced service delivery or lowered costs in the private incarceration industry. In fact, studies in this area are inconclusive, beginning with the first challenge of how to establish equivalence in any analysis. Private prison corporations seek out prison populations that are easier to handle, again not unlike insurance 'cream skimming' in the healthcare sector. On questions of cost-savings, therefore, they are difficult to compare to public prison populations. Equally unimpressive have been studies measuring quality indicators, where private prisons perform no better, and often worse, than their public counterparts. In a meta-study on such indicators, Brett Burkhardt (2019a) has concluded that private prisons are outperformed their public counterparts on matters of inmate misconduct, public safety, employee skills and training, staff turnover, inmate work assignments, and inmate grievances. And they fail to better public institutions on inmate assaults, staff safety, staffing levels, healthcare for inmates, remedial court orders, and inmate recidivism (2019a, p. 203). This is the quantitative data—the qualitative evidence is far more damning. Shane Bauer (2018), a journalist who went inside a Core-Civic facility undercover as a low-paid prison guard, revealed a world that was unregulated, grotesque, and barbaric. With unattended medical problems, no educational services, ill-equipped and sparsely populated guards, and a non-rehabilitative culture, he describes a world of violence and inhumanity. Bauer, subsequently, purchased his way into a CoreCivic shareholder's meeting (with the purchase of one share), where executives described the company's core mission, 'to serve the public good'.

As an important note, the extractive elements of prisons are evident in more than the comparative evaluation of private *versus* public facilities. The entire incarceration system is a complex organization, with a series of necessary tasks beyond those performed by correctional officers. From laundry to food supply to telecommunications, both public and private prisons have spawned infrastructural services that go far beyond the prison as a holding facility. Indeed, the utilization of the term prison-industrial complex is intended to include this reality, as a host of service providers extract pecuniary gain from the basic necessities of the prison population. While not directly the subject of this chapter, their presence is worth noting, as they speak to a culture of cost-cutting, privatization, subcontracting, and price-gouging that has permeated the entire public endeavour of incarceration. Prisons have opened the door to private providers, who make millions off of everyday necessities, including utensils, laundry, and even prison-suitable pens. Telephone companies have gained a lock hold on entire regions of incarceration, charging prisoners and their families exorbitant rates for calls, garnering billions in revenues. Commissary services also pull in billions, providing meager food additions to prisoners for a price. All of this can be facilitated by JPay, a company providing those related to and outside the prison population the ability to send funds electronically, enabling both enhanced purchasing and hefty service fees. Finally, healthcare, free to prisoners, involves companies making billions in revenues for service delivery that has come under severe scrutiny and legal challenge for its poor quality (Eisen, 2019, pp. 87–90).

In a similar manner, prison corporations have demonstrated themselves to be considerably nimble in the evolving political environment of criminal justice, as well as the fit-and-start funding of prison reform. These corporations recognized early in their tenure that the primary means of accumulation—incarceration—would be vulnerable to the push and pull of politics, making alternative and evolving revenue sources a necessity. Here, Immigration and its increasing criminalization has proven to be low hanging fruit. There has been, since the Bush administration, a very clear turn to nativism in US policy, adhered to relentlessly during the Obama years, and put on steroids during the Trump administration. Along with this, "immigration is framed as a severe threat, a multidimensional one that endangers national identity and social cohesion ... [which] became increasingly nuanced once terrorism was added to the existing rhetoric" (Moreno and Price, 2018, p. 158). Even after the Obama administration initiated its incarceration reforms in 2009, Department of Homeland Security (DHS) detention of non-citizens grew by 25 percent while cases for illegal entry into the U.S. amounted to half the federal criminal cases by 2015 (Eisen, 2019, p. 173). As Moreno and Price (2018) have argued, immigration, like the war on drugs, has been subject to increasing 'securitization', where detention has become an attractive feature of prison corporations' accumulation strategies (2018, pp. 144–145). As with conventional forms of incarceration, intensified political rhetoric at the national level bears concrete opportunities on the ground, which have come to constitute an important component of these corporations' profit strategies.

The immigrant population detained in private facilities amounts to a much higher proportion than in conventional incarceration—over 75 percent. The average daily number of these private detainees rose over 400 percent in the two decades previous to the Trump administration, after which it spiked precipitously.

Not surprisingly, then, the number of private facilities operating for the DHS has also surpassed 75 percent, with over half of those in custody held by just two corporations: GEO and CoreCivic (Ahmed, 2019). The corporate attraction to immigration has grown over this period for distinct reasons, not the least of which is the dollar value of federal immigration contracts in comparison to other sources. Given the *per diem* ceiling on profitability, the fact that federal contracts pay out at twice the level for immigration detainees, corporate gravitation to this field is to be expected. Daniel Stageman (2013) has suggested that in the overall political economy of punishment, immigration offers compelling possibilities for profit. For these corporations, "even if we make the generous assumption that immigrant detainees are twice as expensive to house as traditional prisoners, they still represent a 'clientele' with the potential to more than double [the] operating margin per compensated person-day, making the detention market an attractive one indeed" (2013, p. 228). Federal contracts are also considerably more stable than the patchwork of local and state arrangements that make up the bulk of the prison market. Congressional funds are stable in a manner that local funds—subject to balanced budget constraints and restricted sources of revenue—cannot be. Little wonder that the proportion of federal contracts for GEO, CoreCivic, and MTC now amount to roughly 50 percent of their revenues, more than half of which comes from immigration detention (Ahmed, 2019).

It is important to note, as well, that immigration is uniquely profitable, because the public role being performed is limited to detention. The societal objectives of public incarceration, as suggested above, ostensibly carries both punitive and rehabilitative content, and the moral treatment of those incarcerated should, ostensibly, be something more than a cost 'input'. But in the securitized 'threat' environment of immigration detention, the responsibility of private detention facilities towards non-citizens is far more limited. As Eisen (2019) has pointed out, those detained possess little in the way of legal rights, and there is rarely anything akin to "programmatic services such as education, mental health or drug abuse counseling, or job training" (2019, p. 176). As in the case of conventional prisons, corporate actors envision their role as emulating the tasks of federal and/or local officials, but at a fixed, negotiated price. And the reality is that federal officials do not see immigration detention as actual incarceration or prison, a designation that would imply the need for a greater number of services and legal entitlement. Adaptive accumulation discourages these actors from going beyond the bare minimum, as this would neither conform to the prevailing political culture on immigration (more on this below) nor adhere to the obvious business model that minimizes costs against stipulated contract rates. These facilities are treated not as prisons, but rather has holding centers: "[they] are a hybrid form of detention, somewhere between county jail and federal prison"

(2019, p. 183). Consequently, minimal service features and corral-like detention facilities project a rather inhumane imagery, reaching extreme proportions during the scandals of the Trump administration, with family separation and detained children taking center stage. CoreCivic, in reaction to such imagery, attempted a defamation suit against the activists who publicized its involvement in the Trump administration's forced family separation (ostensibly a deterrent to illegal immigration). The case was thrown out, however, as the court found that the corporation (along with GEO and MTC) plainly and publicly cooperated with the program, housing the parents whom had been separated from their own children (Pauly, 2020).

As private incarceration and detention have become increasingly unpalatable, the adaptive strategies of these corporations nonetheless proceed. There is certainly an understanding within the industry that the expansionary nature of incarceration cannot, in the long run, endure. The Obama administration issued an executive order extinguishing federal private contracts on prisons, which was reversed by the Trump administration, and has now been resuscitated by the Biden administration. This political to-and-fro is highly evident to corporate officials, evident in their qualifying statements to shareholders. Even if the existing long-term contracts are honoured, and even if state-level incarceration contracts do not immediately recede, these actors foresee a necessity to modify their extractive business model. Burkhardt (2019a) refers to a SEC filing by CoreCivic (at the time, CCA) to highlight prevailing industry fears:

> Resistance to privatization of correctional and detention facilities ... could result in our inability to obtain new contracts, the loss of existing contracts, or other unforeseen consequences. The operation of correctional and detention facilities by private entities has not achieved complete acceptance by either governments or the public (2019b, p. 403).

As a pre-emptive response, corporations have initiated a sectoral expansion across the spectrum of criminal justice, an extractive strategy that targets an even larger population. GEO and CoreCivic have sought to broaden their activities, focusing on the wider market of community supervision and re-entry. In 2018, there were 4.4 million people under community supervision in the U.S., twice the prison population, and roughly 8.5 times the comparable European average (Bradner *et al.*, 2020). As this population is decreasing at a rate far more slowly than prison populations, it represents an appealing lateral market for the incarceration industry, with its attraction to any government largesse that can be translated into private revenues.

Adaptation has taken multiple forms, in this regard, such as GEO creating a GEO Care division that deals with residential treatment, youth services, electronic monitoring and community based correctional services. Increasingly, rehabilitative services and those oriented towards parole and probation are making up a larger and larger segment of GEO revenues. Even as the Trump administration exhibited a positive governmental disposition towards incarceration, GEO's community services had already grown to 18 percent of its total revenues (Eisen, 2019, p. 234). By 2017, CoreCivic had spent some $270 million on acquiring residential re-entry facilities around the country, with an eye to vertical integration and rebranding (Takei, 2017). The obvious difficulty here lies in the fact that probation and parole systems in the U.S. have been subject to heavy criticism for their unfairness, inequalities, and direct connection back to the carceral system. In 2018, 28 percent of those locked up were for reasons of violation of parole or probation, and if only state prisons are considered, the figure climbs to 45 percent. A very large proportion of such reimprisonments stem from technical, non-criminal trigger violations, feeding mass incarceration, rather than limiting it (Frankel and Pitter, 2020, pp. 1–3). This raises the prospect that the nature and purpose of re-entry programs are becoming subject to a glaring conflict of interest. The very companies that stand to gain from violations are the same parties that would assess violations. This does not just "keep people in prison, but ... keep[s] people involved in the criminal justice system generally, whether through expanding the populations subject to probation, extending probation terms, or returning people to prison through probation revocations" (Takei, 2017, p. 175). Ultimately, especially in eras of political reform, corporate actors not only defend existing streams of profitability, they also carve out new areas from which private gain can be procured from public revenues.

6.3 Government, Public Policy, and Incarceration

Much of this sector hangs on the political context, whether local, state or federal. The political issue of mass incarceration in America will not be solved in the short-term, and corporate actors have proven adept at navigating the public policy it continues to generate. This requires, though, the acquiescence—often enthusiasm—of policy officials, who regularly collaborate in realigning government policy. While government prison contracts had been around for a long time, the Reagan administration gave them the imprimatur of the Oval Office, with the President's Commission on Privatization in 1986 (Eisen, 2019, p. Ch.2). In keeping with the era's prevailing mood, the report called for the potential privatization of a range of governmental services, listing both prisons and immigration as candidates. This endorsed at a federal level what was already underway at the state level, beginning with Tennessee's private prison construction in 1984. It tapped into an emerging government mentality of 'new public management', in which "many jurisdictions have sought to establish privatized arrangements due to [the] potential to cope with increasing expenditures, induce administrative efficiency, lower costs, and provide a better quality of service delivery" (Mitchell and Butz, 2019, p. 509). Importantly, as with other forms of adaptive accumulation, such determinations should be understood as something more than mere outsourcing. Both governmental and corporate actors view these arrangements as an *extension* of government operations, with the assumption that corporate actors can execute all the facets of accountability, transparency and qualitative objectives that should properly inhabit public policy execution.

There are multiple reasons for public policymakers entering into incarceration contracts, and they are executed in varying ways, but certain common themes in this process are worth highlighting. The first of these is the **search for efficiencies and cost savings.** When governments stepped up contracting in the 1980s and 1990s, it was undoubtedly a manifestation of intensifying law-and-order policies, combined with changes in sentencing, which were filling prisons beyond capacity. This could, of course, have led to an expansion of existing public facilities, but that would have fallen out of step with political trends of that period.

> ... [A] factor that catalyzed the industry [was] the maturation of the fiscal conservativism movement that began in the 1970s. As fiscal conservatives claimed policy victories on the national level, states were expected to take on increased responsibilities. But at the same time federal responsibilities were devolving to the states, citizens demanded protection from state tax increases, frequently imposing constitutional restrictions on taxing and borrowing. When states encountered the recession of the early 1980s, these new revenue constraints led to profound turmoil in government budgeting. Private prisons benefited from the movement in two ways. First, despite the overall pressure to reduce spending, prisons often enjoyed favored status due to public fear of crime and the ability of the state to justify public safety as an essential governmental function. Second, even though incarceration as a concept received favored political status, fiscal constraints made borrowing for new construction difficult—thus privatization emerged as a popular alternative. This popularity depended on the notion that contract facilities would avoid the need for state borrowing or expansion of public pay rolls. At the same time, by expanding prison capacity through private facilities, policy-makers could claim cost savings through private sector 'innovations' (Raher, 2010, pp. 217–218).

Whether such efficiencies can be meaningfully identified as a cost saver to government is severely in question. It is certainly true that prison corporations have been able to translate incarceration into a profitable undertaking, but whether that has had positive budgetary effects for federal or state authorities is not obvious. From a new public management perspective, any benefits of government contracting depend on quantitative outcomes: does the utilization of private incarceration lower overall costs for government? Existing literature suggests either extremely weak savings, or no savings at all, while also failing to bring about any kind of 'competitive effect' across the entire carceral domain (Burkhardt, 2019a, p. 211). One nationwide analysis suggested that, for a range of reasons (decreased negotiating leverage, recidivism, escape rates, built-in incarceration incentives, etc.): "state correctional expenditures are not found to be systematically affected by increasing the percent of prisoners in private prisons. Contracting private companies to run prisons does not produce the results that are expected when allowing private markets to allocate resources" (White, Pena and Weiler, 2020, p. 13).

Nonetheless, government actors have not only facilitated the growth of the industry, they have defended it legislatively. At the outset of the 2000s, the industry was facing considerable profitability pressure, as contracts for prisoners were not being procured quickly enough to meet the accelerated building investments of the previous decade. CoreCivic (then CCA) had spiraled to near-bankruptcy, as the speculative demand of the 1990s procured empty facilities and disdain from shareholders. The US government threw a lifeline to the industry in the form of market coordination. Up until this point, most arrangements in the industry had been through direct contracts with state governments or the federal government to build capacity and house inmates directly. But the extensive overhang of facilities stemming from speculative expansion generated the possibility of inter-state facility usage, something which came to be heavily supported at the federal level. With underlying legislation from Congress, the Department of Justice created the Office of the Federal Detention Trustee (OFDT) in 2000. It was given responsibility to manage detainees and coordinate their detention, and it was authorized to use all available facilities—including non-federal—to do so (Raher, 2010, p. 222). This would include all detainees from the Bureau of Prisons (BOP), the US Marshals Service (USMS) and, very significantly, the Immigration and Naturalization Service (now ICE).

The Trustee existed only until 2011, at which point it was folded into the USMS, but its decade-long run actively shaped a 'national market' in beds and facilities that "played a crucial role in the constructive federal bailout of the industry" (2010, p. 222). It created a far more consistent, higher-paying, and reliable revenue flow for an industry that was managing a patchwork of state-contractor deals across the country. By introducing the Detention Services Network (DSNetwork), the Trustee tendered bids on beds and/or facilities that met the need of its affiliated agencies, and it put direct competitive pressure on state governments to meet the higher *per diem* rates set at the federal level. It should be said that these tenders were only nominally competitive, crafted in such a way that they could only be filled by dominant industry actors (GEO, CoreCivic, and MTC). As such, the fortunes of these corporate players very quickly rebounded. The national market, in particular in immigration detention, has extended a helping hand to this industry throughout the Bush, Obama, and Trump administrations. The use of Criminal Alien Requirements (CAR), whereby the serving of pre-deportation, low-security criminal sentences are arranged by the BOP, has been particularly lucrative, occasioning the dramatic growth in low-cost, non-citizen prisoners, guaranteeing the stable conversion of public to private revenues. This market security extends beyond criminal immigrant incarceration more broadly into immigrant detention. In 2010, through an appropriations amendment, the so-called bed mandate was created, calling on DHS to maintain 34000 detainee beds at all times, roughly doubling its hitherto capacity. Three quarters of these beds are maintained privately, and they are paid out at federal rates, regardless of occupancy (Sinha, 2017). The cost, $2.3 billion in 2018, represents more than a quarter of overall industry revenues. While the appropriations amendment has been dropped since 2017, the numbers, unsurprisingly, have grown well in excess of 40,000 as a daily norm, reaching 52,000 in the last year of the Trump Administration (Aleaziz, 2019).

The growth of a national market has undoubtedly intensified problems in an already plagued incarceration and detainment system. When prisoners are moved across state lines and shuffled around as 'units' in a national market, circumstances are made more tense for all parties involved, inside and outside of facilities. Besides the upward pressure on *per diem* rates that have a systemic fiscal effect, out-of-state prisoners are "less happy when serving time far away from family and friends, [and] housing inmates from different jurisdictions (who are subject to different administrative regulations) in one facility often breeds tension" (Raher, 2010, p. 220). Moreover, monitoring from state authorities in this situation is demonstrably worse. Facilities that serve the national market receive a quarter of the monitoring hours that in-state facilities do, while actual contract monitors for such facilities receive a quarter of the job-specific training compared to those dealing with in-state facilities (221).

All of this goes to a second common theme of government involvement in this field of adaptive accumulation: **weak regulatory behaviour.** The ambiguous positioning of private prisons, somewhere between opaque market actor and open adherent to national incarceration standards, places considerable importance on the political (legislative) monitoring of fair and humane treatment of those imprisoned or detained. By all accounts, however, federal and state political actors have not, collectively, sought to invigorate a regulatory and monitoring system that would achieve such ends.

As the growth of private prisons and detention facilities reached a frenzy during the Bush Administration, Congressional members sought access to information that might lead to better regulatory objectives. But information—the lifeblood of any regulatory undertaking—is precisely the item that corporate actors seek to protect, and policymakers seem willing to concede. Blanket legislation, which would rein in the operation of private prisons at a state level, could not advance in Congress. The 2001 introduction of S.842 sought to limit federal grants to states upon "assurances to the Attorney General that if selected to receive funds ... the applicant shall not contract with a private contractor or vendor to provide core correctional services related to the incarceration of an inmate" (US Congress, Senate, 2001, sec.3(a)). That this met with no action (the bill failed) on the part of the Congress is not surprising, but the subsequent and consistent failure to demand even adequate regulatory information highlights the depth of political unwillingness to hold industry publicly accountable. Since 2005, legislation has been introduced in every Congress that would require private contractors to comply with same standards of any government agency in relation to the Freedom of Information Act (FOIA). The latest instantiation of this, H.R.5087, requires that a non-governmental "record relating to a prison, correctional or detention facility shall be ... subject to [the FOIA], to the same extent as if the record was maintained by an agency operating a Federal prison, correctional, or detention facility" (US Congress, House, 2019, sec.3(a)). In fact, this string of Congressional bills has only ever advanced to the stage of committee hearings once, in 2008, with every other Congress allowing such bills simply to languish. For that hearing, CoreCivic (then CCA) submitted written testimony, suggesting that this bill was a "solution in search of a problem" that would, unnecessarily and unfairly, "impose upon the private sector an unprecedented requirement to respond directly to requests for information to the greater public" (US Congress, House, 2008, para.12–13). Ultimately, the source of Congressional resistance is laid out clearly in this hearing: Ranking member Louie Gohmert (R-TX) captures predominantly Republican objections to "singling out private prisons to bear the burden of FOIA obligations by asserting that housing prisoners is a core and a unique governmental service" (2008, para.17). However, the assertion that a core governmental service *was* and *is* being carried out by CoreCivic, GEO, and MTC is, in fact, almost impossible to deny. Nevertheless, these corporations would not, and have not, become subject to such transparency requirements—an obligation which all governmental correctional agencies must fulfill.

The unwillingness on the part of legislators to hold corporate subcontractors accountable as full agents of government speaks to the central dilemma around adaptive accumulation related to public sovereignty. It is precisely that "these quasi-government relationships are often plagued by complicated issues around the government delegating core public responsibilities" (Eisen, 2019, p. 55). And industry actors have been selectively willing to take up this role, speaking far less about outright privatization and more about public-private partnerships.

> Recently, the industry has presented itself *as* true public servants. For example, CoreCivic's core mission, as stated on its home webpage, is to 'better the public good', GEO Group on its home page, says 'GEO believes we can and should have a positive impact on the community we serve.' On its homepage, MTC prominently declares itself 'a leader in social impact'. Both CoreCivic and GEO have reorganized and rebranded in ways to emphasize their public mission, with divisions dedicated to 'Community, Safety, and properties, respectively (Burkhardt, 2019b, p. 409).

Quite clearly, however, when it comes to issues of accountability, transparency, and regulatory applicability, these same operators wish to hoist their private, market credentials, referencing trade secrecy or security concerns as primary counterarguments. In general, federal and state policymakers have conventionally gone along with this dual reality, extending exemptions or special status to government contractors in relation to public disclosure of records, on the premise that it exposes contractors' wider business model to marketplace competitors, hurting the company itself and distorting the broader market. In the case of private incarceration, however, Stephen Raher (2010) has suggested that such claims possess a faulty logic. First, he argues that governments are the *only* customers in an oligopolistic sector, and the likelihood of any 'market distortion' is fanciful, at best. Additionally, he argues that there are no substantial trade secrets in the prison industry. Trade secrecy should be extended only to matters that are valuable, secret, and definitively advantageous, none of which applies to this sector, where incarceration methods are known or easily ascertainable (2010, p. 237). Yet the disposition of federal and state actors toward regulatory principles for private prisons—anticipating their needs as fully-fledged market participants—remains undisturbed to date.

Given their fiscal and legal functions, legislatures are critical in this arrangement, but so too are executive administrations that organize the use of funds and administer agency-related contracts. This relates to a third prevailing theme: the **susceptibility of the industry to administrative decisions, rooted in popular political sentiment.** More recent history suggests that the executive arm of the state can have a decisive effect on the viability of the industry, and that the industry is both vulnerable and responsive to executive action. The disposition of executive offices are themselves, of course, highly influenced by the political leanings of their inhabitants. It was, for instance, the conservative Bush Department of Justice that expressed hesitance over the putative costs to taxpayers from increased access to information requests, which, in turn, contributed to Congressional inaction in the 2008 legislative process. Moreover, that same administration created the DHS, and its ramping up of immigrant detention greatly bolstered the fortunes of industry actors, particularly CoreCivic (then CCA). Similarly, at least on the immigrant detention front, the Obama administration did little to alter this trajectory. Only under political pressure, following the issuance of the DOJ Investigator General's Report in 2016, did Deputy Attorney General Sally Yates announce that the DOJ would be directing the BOP not to renew its contracts on the 13 privately-run federal prison facilities. And this pressure eventually found its way to DHS, as Secretary Jeh Johnson announced an Advisory Council, "to evaluate whether the immigration detention operations conducted by Immigration and Customs Enforcement should move in the same direction" (quoted in Eisen, 2019, p. 179). The BOP process and a potential DHS policy change would have been carried out on a long-term basis, phasing federal facilities out through attrition, and its industrial effects might have only been muted by the reality that the majority of earnings still come from state-based contracts held by these corporations. Still, there can be no doubt that it constituted a political broadside that put the industry in a considerably defensive position.

As such, there could have been no greater historical windfall for the industry than the election of the Trump administration. Given the pronouncement by the 2016 Clinton campaign that it would make good on the existing DOJ policy intentions, the prospects for accumulation looked increasingly problematic, particularly in the face of a 'negative trend' in immigrant detention. You would not know this by the words of CoreCivic (then CCA) CEO, Damon Hininger, who proclaimed "... that being around thirty years and being in the operation in many, many states, and also doing work with the federal government going back to the 1980s, where you had [a] Clinton White House, you had a Bush White House, you had [an] Obama White House, we've done very, very well" (quoted in Eisen, 2019, p. 148). This equanimity proved prescient, as the surprise election of Trump–and his accompanying anti-immigrant rhetoric—turned the tide dramatically. Executive orders were reversed, and while the overall numbers of federal prisoners followed its incremental decline, the percentage held by private prison corporations did not, stabilizing between 8 and 9 percent. More importantly, the upswing in federal detention of immigrants at border facilities accelerated considerably, as the administration's follow-through on campaign declarations demanded new facilities. Unsurprisingly, stock shares in CoreCivic and GEO jumped following the 2016 election, demonstrating investor confidence in the continuing availability of 'carceral markets' when the appropriate administration was in charge (Collingwood, Morin and El-Khatib, 2018).

With this change in political tone, the executive arm of government moved swiftly to reverse the existing downward trend in immigrant arrest and deportations. It should be noted, however, that both never reached the 2012 peak achieved by the Obama administration, pointing to the Democrats' own brand of harsh immigration tactics (Gramlich, 2020). Despite this, the posturing of the Trump administration was more on the border itself than internal to communities, reaching a frenzy in 2019, with border apprehension increasing by 100 percent over previously consistent years. The critical quantitative change came in the policy towards detention, expanding dramatically and proving an accumulative goldmine for corporations that hold the strong majority of this population. Daily detentions grew rapidly over the course of the administration, with an average held by ICE in 2019 exceeding 50,000 per day, with another 20,000 by Customs and Border Patrol (CPB) and 11,000 children with Health and Human Services (HHS) (Serwer, 2019). Facility expansion has involved primarily large 'processing centers' operated by private corporations, as well as contracted local and county jails across the country. With this surge has come predictable criticism of monitoring and conditions of detention. DHS's own OIG highlighted both problems in two separate reports in 2018 and 2019. In monitoring, the OIG concluded that ICE's procedures "do not ensure adequate oversight or systemic improvements in detention conditions, with some deficiencies remaining unaddressed for years." (US Department of Homeland Security, Office of the Inspector General, 2018, para.1). After on-site inspections of four separate ICE detention facilities, three of them run by GEO corporation, the OIG's conclusions were far more damning:

> Although the conditions varied among the facilities and not every problem was present at each, our observations ... revealed several common issues. [We] observed immediate risks or egregious violations of detention standards at facilities in Adelanto, CA, and Essex County, NJ, including nooses in detainee cells, overly restrictive segregation, inadequate medical care, unreported security incidents, and significant food safety issues .... All four facilities had issues with expired food, which puts detainees at risk for food-borne illnesses. At three facilities, we found that segregation practices violated standards and infringed on detainee rights. Two facilities failed to provide recreation outside detainee housing units. Bathrooms in two facilities' detainee housing units were dilapidated and moldy. At one facility, detainees were not provided appropriate clothing and hygiene items to ensure they could properly care for themselves. Lastly, one facility allowed only non-contact visits, despite being able to accommodate in-person visitation. Our observations confirmed concerns identified in detainee grievances, which indicated unsafe and unhealthy conditions to varying degrees at all of the facilities we visited (US Department of Homeland Security, Office of the Inspector General, 2019, para.1).

There should be no mistaking what this means for corporations active in immigration detention, repulsive as such outcomes might be. Lax conditions, overcrowding, insufficient monitoring, or any other poorly provided resources all translate into stronger accumulation prospects, higher profits and satisfied shareholders. The parameters of adaptive accumulation have, in this regard, never been so palpable: expanding government programs; private execution of public service; and a hyper-validation of market principles through weak regulatory reach and poor qualitative outcomes. The administration's turn in 2019 to weaken National Detention Standards (NDS) further at 140 facilities in 44 states can only intensify this dynamic and make future reforms more difficult (Cho, 2020).

The Biden administration's announcement of re-establishing the abovementioned attrition policy on private incarceration contracts in federal prisons is an impactful, albeit complicated, development. All the same problems with existing contracts (with both private facilities and local officials) remain intact, and the administration has made no concomitant announcement regarding immigrant detention. Not surprisingly, David Garfinkle, CoreCivic's Executive Vice President and Chief Financial Officer, expressed confidence in the political situation going forward:

> [When] you think of all the other initiatives that are on [the President's] plate, healthcare, tax reform, climate change, trade negotiations, it's probably a while before you would expect the focus to become on private prisons. It's just such a complex area to solve because we provide such an essential governmental service there that I just can't believe that, that would be one that they want to tackle out of the box (quoted in Simon, 2021, para.13).

While the administration defied this outlook, with an initial executive order in January 2021, reinstating the Obama policy, Garfinkle is not wrong on immigration and state detention (together comprising some 80 percent of private industry's revenues), where the matter will not be so straightforward to address. Even the parts that it does address–non-renewal of contracts by BOP and USMS–will be an incremental subtraction of industry profits, but the order does nothing to prevent a parallel expansion of corporate strategies around post-detention surveillance and re-entry, or even expansion of state contracts in select locales.

This raises a final prevailing theme for public decision making: **the inextricability of local policy.** At both state and local/municipal levels of government, non-federal officials are heavily tied into the private system of detention, not only as a matter of short-term budgeting frugality, but also as a matter of perceived local job loss and economic development. GEO alone has contracts in 11 separate states, and the ebb and flow of its prison and detention revenues have palpable effects on the politico-economic context of states and municipalities. As mentioned above, many state constitutions place legislatures under balanced budget requirements, which heavily affect both their state prison system and the overall fiscal largesse that can be directed toward smaller communities. As such, the prospect of private—or any other—facilities, requiring paid personnel and sub-contracted commercial support (laundry, transportation, etc.), translates into material sustenance for these communities, and the extraction of property tax often represents a lifeline for municipal revenues.

One of many examples can be highlighted in Colorado, where state legislators recently adjusted language in a bill originally designed to wean the state off of the use of private correctional facilities. Representatives of industry (CoreCivic), in cooperation with citizens and officials from the two affected counties, lobbied legislators on the necessity of these facilities to their community. Local commissioners argued that these facilities are such a significant part of local tax revenues (54% for Crowley Country and 25% for Bent County) that closures would bankrupt the local administrations. Moreover, community members insisted publicly that these facilities made up some of the only economic prospects that citizens had, without which the likelihood of a demographic exodus would greatly increase. Not only did this impress legislators enough to change the language in the proposed state study, but they also amended the legislation to grant the Governor final decision-making power on out-of-state prisoner contracts with a third private facility in Burlington. Clearly zeroing in the problematic nature of a commodified trade in prisoners, legislators, nonetheless, defaulted to language that directed the Governor's approval not to be 'unreasonably withheld' (Goodland, 2020).

Such stories can be repeated through the many states that employ private prison contracts or allow contracting by out-of-state or federal sources. Immigration, in this regard, has constituted a local revenue source not only for private contractors but also in the very maintenance of local public facilities. Originally introduced with the 1996 Immigration and National Act, the 287(g) program embodies a memorandum of agreement that authorizes "state, county, and local law enforcement agencies (LEAs) to enforce federal immigration law" (Stageman, 2013, p. 230). Here, federal authorities direct subsidies to local law enforcement agencies, offering a fiscal stimulus to pay for local incarceration facilities and the maintenance of personnel. The attractiveness of this to local government structures, starved for budgetary sources, cannot be understated. In political economy terms, Stageman (2013) labels this an 'extractive' (rather than exploitive) activity, as states, counties, and municipalities obtain their share of 'profit' to maintain an overall incarceration regime. He notes that this "extractive activity approaches immigrants as analogous to a natural resource: immigrants need only be present in order for the various interests involved in detention operations to profit" (2013, p. 231). This has led to a considerable misuse, as 'offenses' that in no way meet the criteria of a misdemeanour have been used as a pretense for detention and, thus, continued municipal funding. In this sense, a localized, extractive political economy of detainment is maintained that both meets with popular approval—securing employment and facilities while serving as a conservative 'law and order' prop—and greatly dovetails with the immigration activities of corporate players.

Ultimately, government at all levels has progressively drawn itself into the many facets of private incarceration. And, having reached a certain level of intricate involvement, extrication from that process will prove difficult on both a logistical and political level. It is important to recall this significant feature of adaptive accumulation: ostensible advocates of market performance seek a larger and more complicated share of a paradoxically expanding government pie. As governments take any political action which may reverse or undo this trend (as in the case of the Biden administration), they risk a not-so-surprising number of reverberations from other levels of government and the wider political culture. In other words, the more extensive the public role of private actors has become, the more politically difficult it is to unwind.

6.4 Politico-Cultural Undercurrents: Conditioning Incarceration

The political culture in which adaptive accumulation proceeds is central, because it makes up, in part, the very conditions which corporate agents harness to secure sought-after government revenues. In the case of incarceration, this recalls the familiar politics of 'crisis' and encroaching 'danger' (evident in healthcare and education), but it also taps into deep strains of racial and xenophobic animus that is entwined in the American social fabric. Political economy has always struggled with the integration of the affective and cultural elements of politics into its analysis, but here its interwoven centrality exposes social sentiments, behaviours, and institutional structures that generate the possibility of adaptive accumulation in the first place.

On a budgetary and societal level, 'crisis' has been used as a rhetorical driving force in the growth of prisons for some time. Since the 1980s, increased incarceration rates remain unrelated to crime rates, but they are very highly related to skin colour (Ladipo, 2001). As one of the more trenchant social critiques has made clear, the prison system needs to be seen outside of the 'crime and punishment' paradigm. Instead, the extraordinary incarceration rates for Black and Hispanic populations signal "the obsolescence of the ghetto as a device for caste control and the correlative need for a substitute apparatus for keeping (unskilled) African Americans 'in their place', i.e. in a subordinate and confined position in physical, social, and symbolic space" (Wacquant, 2001, p. 97). Various incantations of the 'war on crime' and 'war on drugs', along with increasingly militarised policing, have fully racialized criminality, rendering an image of 'dangerous' populations, entirely divorced from their socio-economically deprived context (Davis, 1998). This decontextualized projection of 'danger', grafted especially onto black and brown communities, continues to advance a perception of crisis in both criminality and community safety.

In this 'crisis' context, a dual dynamic of punishment (incarceration) and renewal (law and order) underwrites adaptive accumulation, and it finds continuing reinforcement in both the criminal justice system and popular renditions of criminality (such as those in the media). This is readily on display in policing policies, where descending violent crime rates are nonsensically matched with ascending public support for increasing public investment in law-and-order policies. Moreover, the gross imbalance in enforcement and punishment directed at black and Hispanic communities, such as those used in targeted and irrational sentencing laws, has proceeded for decades, in clear sight. Utilising Frommian material psychoanalysis, Leonidis Cheliotis (2013) has questioned why, "crime, or at least certain types of crime, carry attributes that render them publicly more compelling and thereby politically more suitable than other dangers" (2013, p. 251). The answer, he argues, is that a material insecurity besetting the so-called middle class is continuously 're-branded' and displaced onto a narrative of violent street crime. Such danger is personified into minority groups in a manner that:

> ... feeds on the symbolic order of neoliberal capitalism. More specifically, the perpetrators of violent street crime are said and thought to be enjoying instant access to material and ontological gains, from the goods they seize to unrestricted spatial mobility through taking over streets. Thereby induced among the middle classes is the sense of unfairness one consciously feels when others 'short circuit the whole marketplace of effort and reward, when they are perceived as getting exactly what they want without any effort at all—or, more precisely, exactly what you want and can only achieve with great effort' (2013, p. 263).

Here, the road to redemption through punitive institutions is all too clear: substantial popular support for incarceration alleviates the republic of its flawed elements, caricatured as unproductive and undeserving. And as the ranks of prisons have swelled, incarceration has undoubtedly come to be seen as an actuarial rather than rehabilitative project (De Giorgi, 2007). Ultimately, then, the entry of capital as a management and profit-taking endeavour fits seamlessly into this neoliberal logic, targeting and marginalising black and brown 'dangerous classes', undermining opposition and giving rise to a political economy of punishment that 'pays for itself'.

The outcomes of such a political economy, interwoven with racial animus, has provoked powerful resistance, from the civil rights movement to the L.A. riots to Black Lives Matter. But it has also given rise to both the ongoing hyper-militarization of law enforcement and the continuing disproportional and racialized character of incarceration. African Americans are 5 times more likely to be in state prisons than white Americans, and in 5 states, the odds are 10 to 1. Forty percent of state prisoners are black while 21 percent are Hispanic and 35 percent are white (Nellis, 2016). Black populations have long been slotted into the category of 'security threat', justifying myriad policies that undermine, marginalize, and greatly decrease average life prospects. From a political economy perspective, hyper-incarceration has positioned black populations in such a way that entire subsections of community can be devalued in a capitalist society—marked as 'dangerous' and, more damningly, 'unproductive'. Unfortunately, for Black and Hispanic communities, this physical incarceration is only one part of the cycle of marginalization, as accompanying discrimination extends across a range of other social areas: from education to healthcare to housing (Moreno and Price, 2018, pp. 155–156).

As such, when corporations lobby at the state or federal level for 'secure communities', the undertow of this violent, racialized rhetoric is never very far from the surface. Managerial agents for corporations like GEO and CoreCivic are well aware of this societal dynamic, and seek to tap into an already incarceration-heavy cultural bias. Lobbying is just one manner in which they can do so. In this sense, the "prison industry is an archetyped example of an established industry preventing public-spirited reform because of the incentives of existing stakeholders" (Eisenberg, 2016, p. 79). Lining up with community organizations, prison guard unions, victims' rights groups, and conservative politicians, the dangers of demarcation are made evident to all who will listen. Prison guard unions, for instance, are typically understood to be in opposition to private corporations, due primarily to the latter's avoidance of unionized labour. However, there is no doubt that these same unions do work toward an environment that has "historically preferred more punitive criminal laws and longer sentences .... [And] they ... justify these preferences and necessary to punish 'the bad guys'" (2016, p. 94).

Here, the strange confluence of community 'survival' meets with the forces helping to drive continuing incarceration, all buttressed by a deeply racialized political economy of punitive action and extractive behaviour. In the numerous counties that have taken on incarceration as a form of community economic development, the social capacity to compartmentalize prison administration from the racialized and commodified treatment of inmates has proven resilient. Eisen (2019) documents the local tendency to seek out deals for prison operations—public or private—as a means to maintain economic wherewithal inside the community. Reviewing cases in states as diverse as Montana, Minnesota, Oklahoma, and Colorado, a common theme of rural hope and/or despair emerges around the opening and closing of incarceration facilities:

> The prison closure forced pizza parlors and restaurants to close, unemployment soared, and younger families moved away. Driving around the town of 1,200 on a 20-degree day in December 2015, I felt the desolation. The prison has been closed since early 2010, despite rumors over the years of a contract for federal inmates or that the facility would house incarcerated individuals from California. Roads were potholed, only a few restaurants remained, and the town's one gas station seemed to be the central hub of activity (2019, p. 102).

Towns and counties around the country have come to equate a portion of their existential survival with the ebb and flow of inmate facilities. Indeed, corporate building of speculative prisons (most of the prison construction in the last two decades) has been met with optimism, because it offers the lure of employment and heightened use of local services, carefully compartmentalized from the complicated politics of prisoner commodification, overcrowding, out-of-state prison transfers, and institutional racism.

This compartmentalization effect can reach somewhat surprising proportions, resonating even in communities where one might otherwise expect resistance. Judah Schept (2013) has documented this phenomenon in an anonymized (but real) liberal, midwestern county, home to community leaders who were otherwise highly critical of mass incarceration. In order to solve a local prison overcrowding issue, while also seeking economic redevelopment for the county, these same leaders became involved in the expansion of incarceration facilities they termed the 'justice campus'. Equating their solution with rehabilitation over punishment, "officials mapped the bucolic and collegiate identity of the community onto their proposal for the most drastic expansion of carceral control in county history," articulating a "county carcerality [that] existed outside of, and in resistance to, the practices of mass incarceration that they disdained" (2013, p. 72). Schept also documents the somewhat alarming ways in which racist and classist assumptions concerning crime are carried into this progressivist vision for the community. There exists, in other words, a widespread willingness to disassociate the perceived benefits of economic and daily activity around local prisons from the devastating moral, political, and economic impact of mass incarceration. It is hard to imagine a better available terrain in which private prison corporations can expand and/or contract operations, with reasonable prospects for local support.

A comparable notion of 'danger' and 'threat' has been imported into the discussion around immigration, and this has been rather easily channeled into widespread social resentment. There can be little question that since the first decade of the post-Cold War, and especially after 9/11, immigration has been increasingly positioned as a security threat. Dangerously, this has resulted in "a political landscape in which the manipulation of images ... and ... sensational political rhetoric are used to justify policy responses that are punitive and burdensome ... while also providing the private prison industry with ... a way to maximize this new punitive market of detaining immigrants" (Moreno and Price, 2018, p. 159). This is evidenced in the manner in which local anti-immigrant legislation was spurred on by industry—with the help of the American Legislative Exchange Council—in Arizona (SB1070) and, subsequently, dozens of other states. Such legislation allows for stepped up local detention of immigrants, and the private prison industry clearly recognized its increased accumulation prospects in this environment of local resentment. As such, it has directed some 90 percent of its lobbying resources towards state or sub-state proposals for stricter immigration laws and, especially, detainment policies (2018, p. 145).

No such wave of immigration detention occurs without strong social and political sentiment to host it, with or without the appearance of the Trump administration. There is a two-fold social process emanating from stricter immigration laws that involve both disciplining and resentment. On the former, harsher detention policies, serve to discipline illegal immigrants and, arguably, the immigration community more broadly. Whether 'illegal' or not, the spectre of detention "injects an element of fear into social service contacts, from schooling to healthcare, that encourages self-exclusion ... [It] allows actors in the field to extract profit from social and economic shifts that might otherwise be considered roundly negative" (Stageman, 2013, p. 231). On the latter, waves of high unemployment or sectoral displacement regularly give rise to social tension which, in turn, directs anxiety and resentment towards immigrant communities. This resentment is rationalized, insofar as increased immigration putatively "throws off the balance between the benefits (in terms of lower costs for a variety of goods and services) and detriments (in terms of labour competition and wage depression) that a given community's unauthorized immigrants represents" (2013, p. 232). The politico-cultural outcome is a fusion of the social apprehension of downward economic mobility, on the one hand, and channelled fear of difference, on the other. Community anxiety, even hostility, is something more than 'irrational fear'—it is the popular expression of residual political agency in the face of much broader, overwhelming social forces (global production and distribution networks, manufacturing relocation, geopolitical insecurity, etc.) that govern both local livelihoods and regional immigration trends.

In this sense, whether government offices are inhabited by a Trump or a Trump-like figure makes a difference only in absolute terms. Social sentiments circulating in the political culture for two decades have helped foster a terrain for industry's entry into and expansion of immigrant detention. At the time of writing, the new Biden administration is grappling with the ongoing results of this sentiment, leading to disappointment among immigration advocates that detention policies have been permitted to continue. This is, no doubt, a function of dealing with 'facts on the ground' that were buoyed by previous political rhetoric, but it is also brought about by the Democrats' sensitivity to appearing 'soft' on immigration. Reform efforts around detention are easily countered by Congressional Republicans, like Ted Cruz or Josh Hawley, standing at the border wall in bullet-proof vests, armed CPB personnel at their side. As with incarceration, shifts in the electoral winds may elicit hope for change from critics of private industry, but the latter's adaptive accumulation strategy will remain closely attuned to socio-cultural environments that demonstrate continuing receptivity to heighted law-and-order policies, incarceration, detention, and/or post-detention surveillance.

6.5 Conclusion

Incarceration is a deeply controversial arena of public policy, in which citizens and policymakers alike must ask the simple question: 'how much is enough?'. This is obviously not a question restricted to US society, but the American answer has surely pushed the limits of what is possible in a liberal capitalist democracy. With what can only be described as a harsh and punitive turn in the 1980s, the mass incarceration process has grown to unmanageable levels in the twenty-first century. In this regard, adaptive accumulation has emerged as both public policy crisis management tool and a highly attractive corporate strategy. It is important to reiterate that private industry did not create this incarceration dilemma, and the removal of private operators from the scene will not, on the whole, solve it. It is precisely, however, in that ambiguous outcome that private operators have inserted themselves, heralding the problem-solving character of market procedures while continuously doing their part to expand (or at least maintain) governmental purview in law enforcement, criminal justice, and incarceration/detention facilitation. Government expansion, after all, is good for business and, as it stands, business continues to be good.

This industry, more so than previously discussed sectors, inhabits a deeply problematic moral territory, with its ultimate objective far more closely aligned with quota detention numbers (and *per diem* payments) than with rehabilitation and societal re-entry. That the still swelling ranks of those detained or incarcerated are emblematic of broad American social contradictions—racism, class inequality, police violence, xenophobia—does not, unfortunately, seem to form a significant barrier to adaptive accumulation. Indeed, for all the justified controversy surrounding these matters, they also form part of the basis from which much social anxiety around 'threats', 'fear', 'safety', and 'security' emanate. Add to this political institutions and actors seeking to appear fiscally proactive, unwilling to extend the state apparatus beyond the bare budgetary minimum, and corporate actors have been furnished with another sector in which they can assume a quasi-public role. No doubt, corporate fortunes can turn, as the sector's political sensitivity may send it headlong into meaningful and sustained reform. However, between its present position and this hypothesized future, not only is there a great deal of complicated dismantling of incarceration and detainment systems, but the industry's pre-emptive lateral movement into surveillance and re-entry may *shift but not end* its ongoing quasi-public role. In other words, adaptive accumulation may meet its political limits in this sector, but that does not signal its demise anytime soon.

Chapter 7: Conclusion—Moving Forward in America

The overarching manner in which we depict the politico-economic trajectory of a given time and/or place matters, insofar as its explanatory value brings greater understanding to seemingly disassociated details and events. In this sense, an interpretation of US political economy as neoliberal and, specifically, Anglo-American is surely of value. The latter points to the long-term historical context in which American capitalism has developed since the late 19th century, with its attendant features of individualism, state minimalism, cultural suspicion of government and organizations (including unions), and a belief in the progressive effects of the market as a means to overcome social problems. For its part, neoliberalism, has signaled a critical turn in capitalist industrial relations and public policy, led especially by Anglo-American governments since the 1980s, to reinforce these liberal values but also claw back the income and wealth redistributions of the postwar Keynesian world. That the U.S. has played a central role in this refashioning of capitalism and public policy is undeniable, and growing social inequality, measured in income and wealth—deeply intertwined with race and gender—is testimony to the American version of the 'neoliberal turn'.

Importantly, however, if the advance of this political economy is to be properly understood, our analytical categories must be subject to intermittent review, such that they better capture *all* relevant systemic dynamics, especially those concrete instances which do not fit seamlessly within our prevailing understanding. In the context of the U.S., the interpretation of capital accumulation solely through the lens of Anglo-American neoliberalism can be, in certain respects, misleading. Nestled within this systemic dynamic, a considerable share of corporate attention has been captured by what this work has termed adaptive accumulation. Adaptive accumulation sits counter-intuitively with the usual neoliberal disdain for governmental intervention, shored up by market validation. Instead, the endorsement of market organizing principles remains, but a paradoxical expansion of government programs accompanies it, with an eye to transforming these public revenues into secure private channels of wealth accumulation. Corporate actors and public policymakers alike walk a fine line between amplifying government programs while proclaiming that the market will 'do it better'. Corporations, in fact, proclaim their primary interest in serving the public good while the politicians brandish their fiscal responsibility on behalf of taxpayers. Both of these outcomes are open to serious question, as the case studies in this work have shown, but the unabashed neoliberal faith in market mechanisms forms a reliable backdrop against which such proclamations can persist.

https://doi.org/10.1515/9783110761801-007

At the time of writing, the U.S.—and the world—are entangled in the epidemiological outbreak of COVID-19. This work has purposefully sidestepped the associated temptation to restate continuously the weaknesses of American societal organization through the lens of this singular event. However, it is surely worth noting that the arrival of the COVID pandemic on American soil has rapidly brought to the fore many of the societal contradictions highlighted within adaptive accumulation. As the condition has spread swiftly in waves through the social fabric, the wide variation in state intervention; an ever-present ideological insistence on minimal disturbance to the economy; the effects of inequality on epidemiological spread; and a highly fractionalized and disorganized ensemble of social policies and structures have coalesced in a largely uncontrollable—and socially traumatic—spread of illness and death. It has raised questions over the fundamental unfairness in US society, along class, race, and gender lines, as well as the default sanctity of the market, so prevalent in US political culture. But it has now also motivated one of the largest federal interventions in fiscal and social policy since Roosevelt's New Deal. That the bulk of the pandemic progressed in the final year of the Trump administration made its exposure of festering societal dilemmas all the more controversial and subject to social conflict. And, indeed, many of the contradiction that COVID has pried open occur in the areas of concern here, particularly in healthcare, education, and incarceration, but even in the administration of military personnel and their families.

In this sense, the ailing features of American political economy, so heavily travelled by the SARS-Cov2 virus, are also closely associated to adaptive accumulation. The conclusion from this is difficult to avoid: that though areas of public policy have expanded in size and often scope, their intermingling with adaptive accumulation has left them weaker and more vulnerable to criticism. This work has demonstrated the extraordinary surge in private actors' involvement in military operations and domestic base installations. While corporations brandish their 'serving our soldiers' credentials before Congress, the problematic results of weakening accountability, increased danger to civilian and non-civilians alike, and the devasting impacts of poor housing for military families speaks to a different reality. For its part, healthcare, always a highly uneven field in the U.S., has been particularly attractive public policy for adaptive accumulation. Thus, starting from an already advantageous standpoint for industry, the nominally public roles of private actors have grown through a deeper incursion into Medicare Advantage, certain state Medicaid policies (not examined here), Pharmaceutical care for seniors, and the multiple facets of the ACA that award insurers with a subsidy-driven insurance market which is private in nature but government-organized in the eyes of the public. The profound and growing profit levels of the health industry make these arrangements seem especially obscene.

Following quickly behind, K-12 education makes up a vast field of public revenues for corporations looking to secure returns. This work has flushed out the complicated nature of charterization and its multiple connections to private revenue streams, even when the schools in question are ostensibly 'non-profit'. As with healthcare, so-called educational clientele—students and parents—are ensnared in privately run facilities once they are in place. Who can afford the gap in coverage, chaos, and lost time in health or education which would occur in any policy process of reversal or reform? Public policymakers will not weather the storm of ensuing confusion, popular anger, and necessity for raising taxes, and this reality reinforces the politically secure nature of adaptive accumulation. Similarly, 'facts on the ground' make extricating prisons and detainment facilities from private capital a difficult endeavor, at best. Since the incarceration industry's growth through the 1990s, it has always been an ace card for corporate actors to appeal to racialized images of 'lawlessness' and 'soft on crime' themes, as a not-so-subtle way of drumming up support for public-private contracts. The politico-cultural acceptance of both the market as 'fixer' and the social retribution associated to criminality and immigration means that once created, private facilities are not subject to widespread societal interrogation, review, or reform. In other words, at its worst, the market is thought to save money for taxpayers (rather than citizens), and criminals and/or immigrants (non-citizens) are perceived as getting what they deserve. Policymakers and corporate actors are, in this sense, absolved of responsibility and accountability.

This blind faith in the market and weak cultural attachment to public policy endeavours have helped to expand a conducive environment for adaptive accumulation in US society. The peculiarity of America's politico-cultural constellation cannot be emphasized enough, as it makes the 'adaptive' part of this multi-sectoral accumulation possible in the first place. It is not as if public-private relationships cannot occur without a stronger sense of the public good. Germany, for instance, has utilized associational governance for over a century in critical areas of social policy, not the least of which is in its healthcare system. Here, private (non-profit) actors manage healthcare funds, interacting with corporate organizations (pharmaceuticals, physicians, etc.), all densely regulated by the state. These arrangements, of course, carry their own challenges related to neoliberal trends, but the public objectives of solidarity and social good do continue to prevail (Loeppky, 2014, ch.5). In the U.S., however, the ideological priority afforded to market actors places them in a unique position to continue to claim superior efficacy and social utility, even as their primary orientation is profit, prioritized above broad societal outcomes. Combined with a distrust of things governmental; an often-dramatized display of budget austerity; and a racially-disproportionate validation (even celebration) of societal inequality, adaptive accumulation has come to fit somewhat paradoxically within the deep entrenchment of American neoliberalism. Here, expanding the public domain through the execution of contracts for corporate actors, where the latter derive secure markets and a quasi-public authority, we find an ongoing push for state largesse in the heart of ostensible Anglo-American state minimalism.

With qualifications, this is a bipartisan political dynamic, as both Republican and Democratic policymakers are caught up in the sectoral intricacies explored here. It is fair to argue that Republicans inhabit a kind of prime mover position in these debates. The consistent pattern of Republican administrations that preach austerity, but then 'tax less and spend more' is evident from Reagan to Bush Jr. to Trump, all of whom undermined federal and state revenues while expanding the deficit to previously unseen levels. Republicans, in the end, believe less in fiscal responsibility than the strategic redistribution of real and borrowed social wealth. Corporate actors involved in adaptive accumulation have realized many of their most auspicious gains under these administrations. Democrats, meanwhile, oscillate between the role of 'placeholder', unable to break away from the existing institutional arrangement of market incursion in public policy, and being spellbound by the potential of market-delivered public program expansion. The latter, exemplified most strongly by the Clinton administration, sees Democrats fashioning their policy goals more closely to neoliberal values than even many of their more conservative counterparts. For its part, the Obama administration surely occupied the role of placeholder, struggling to negotiate existing blockages in social policy (healthcare, education) and regulation (financial reform), desperately fighting to get corporate America and Republicans onside while, each time, boxing itself mostly into an expanded version of the status quo. The deft maneuvers of lobbies for the pharmaceutical and healthcare industries in the face of the Affordable Care Act; the financial sector during the emergence and implementation of the Dodd-Frank Act; and the private prison industry in the face of pronouncements at the DOJ are surely indicative of Democrats' relative fecklessness in the face of adaptive accumulation, as well as neoliberal development more generally.

The Trump administration, in important ways, merely brought this all to the surface, albeit in a bombastic and particularly cruel manner. Many of the fights that the administration waged rhetorically—against lawlessness, immigration waves, foreign economic advantage—tapped into deep strains of American political culture. This messaging was not procured by Trump, but its content has, importantly, furnished the conditions for adaptive accumulation in the U.S. for decades. Take Trump's multiple threats to rein in the drug companies' exceptionally high prices, which are, ultimately, a long-term result of successive administrations' efforts to grow US pharma's global economic strength. While there were ongoing threats to bring down drug prices, there was no questioning of the manner in which drug access is written into US law, prohibiting government purchase leveraging in Medicare, Medicaid, or the ACA, effectively outlawing price regulation. Simultaneously, the deference given to big Pharma during the COVID pandemic, largely avoiding any government interventions beyond funding, speaks volumes to the privileged position of the industry in relation to short- and long-term public policy. It is unlikely that Trump possessed any genuine concern for drug prices; rather, he sensed intuitively that this hot-button political issue could enhance his popularity. But the confused ideological reaction by both Republicans and Democrats, each with a hand in building the system that has resulted in sky-high pricing and quasi-public authority for pharmaceutical companies, is testimony to the peculiarity of adaptive accumulation nestled within American neoliberalism. The Trump administration's disparagement of government programs was accompanied, in the end, by its financial endorsement of those same programs—witness the growth of the military budget; the free hand given to the Secretary of Education to grow the Charter movement; and the redirection of funds for immigrant detention. And who can forget the painful admission of the President's systemic unawareness: "Who knew healthcare was so complicated?" Trump poked and prodded at the painful surface results of market actors' strength in relation to public policy goals in US politics, but his administration's ugly handling of these issues should not be confused with their cause.

In the post-Trump setting, with a new Democratic administration, the resolution of issues raised in this work will get no easier. The Biden administration, resolute on surmounting the COVID crisis, will expend a good deal of political capital before ever getting to broad public policy proposals. As the last chapter made clear, the administration's executive action on prisons, while perhaps an indicative sign, will not easily disentangle the presence of private prison companies from either incarceration or immigrant detention. Legislative moves that change the fortunes of these companies in relation to public policy seem, at best, far on the horizon and, at worst, not possible. The central problem, of course, is that the extrication of public policy from existing contracts or government funding arrangements, whether in prisons, education, healthcare or military, require public investment to replace facilities, personnel, and infrastructural support. Some time ago, Jacob Hacker (2002) made the salient point that critics on the right will always possess the political advantage here, as incremental undermining of publicly-oriented, publicly-orchestrated programs is far easier, far more piecemeal, than the reconstruction of such programs, which requires wholesale, upfront, large public investments (and the utilization of tax revenues). The former can be executed tactically, often indirectly, while the latter is usually public and openly makes claim on a considerable share of the social wealth. Similarly, the political rationales for the former are simple and often de-contextualized, limited to proclamations that the government is taking citizens' income or regulating an element of their lives. Those for the latter are complicated: 'yes, your taxes will increase, but ...'. Arguably, the advancement of public policy removed from market activity may depend on Democrats' willingness to engage in tactical, less open political strategies, such as appending program spending increases onto budget reconciliation bills. Unfortunately, there is only so much room for this kind of maneuver (indeed, only so much legislation can be labelled budgetary), and Democrats have typically shown less willingness to be 'ruthless' in the legislative process.

A bigger obstacle to change exists in the overall political-corporate nexus that invests the legislative and policy process. First, bipartisan involvement in adaptive accumulation means that not all Democrats envision social and public policy to be inconsistent with market motives. More significant, however, is the overwhelming presence of corporate influence across the political landscape, from campaign contributions to extensive institutional lobbying to philanthropic interventions to media domination. With this constellation of influence, the image of corporate participation in public policy is shaped and massaged, such that it is ultimately perceived as both benevolent in its objectives and economical in its procedures. The resulting devotion of the political establishment to the efficacy of the market in this context borders on the dogmatic and really only gets seriously interrogated in moments of controversy. In this regard, the already entrenched position of adaptive accumulation in such a wide array of policy programs will be difficult to unwind, and the advent of new programs will not easily escape its shadow.

Take, for example, the future prospects of 'Medicare for All', mentioned above, as a potential policy agenda for US healthcare. This Bernie Sanders-inspired political agenda would, effectively, expand eligibility in the world's largest single-payer healthcare scheme—Medicare—to all Americans. As originally devised, it would feasibly shut out private insurance, except perhaps in a secondary benefits market, and it would grossly equalize healthcare coverage for US citizens. However, as this work has noted, much of currently existing Medicare coverage is not based on straightforward single-payer system, but is instead mediated by private Medicare Advantage plans, considerably popular in those counties statistically healthy enough to enjoy them. Combining the Democrats' fear of taking things away in healthcare ('you won't have to give up your existing plan') and the assured lobbying, media, and legislative onslaught that such a proposal will provoke, it seems virtually unthinkable that widespread single-payer system could emerge in any meaningful public format. It is hardly surprising that other 2020 Democratic Presidential candidates either started to bend their message ('Medicare for All Who Want It?') or rejected its premise as ill-suited to American political culture. The straightforward simplicity of such a program, building on an already popular public policy, should be an attractive political strategy for Democrats. Yet set in the terrain of adaptive accumulation, the barriers and struggle involved in its execution quickly start to be perceived as political suicide.

In a strong sense, though, Sanders' fight is the fight of all Americans, whether his particular political agenda resonates or not. Steep inequality in the U.S., plagued by poverty, racial inequities, and violence, has proven corrosive to the body politic in ways unimagined only decades ago. That the U.S. remains an outlier among industrial countries in much of its public policy is a profound contributor to this state of being. The basic securities of healthcare and education —underwritten by public revenues, applied universally and equitably to all— alone would do more to advance the well-being of US citizens across the wealth and income spectrum than any past or present political program. But such programs, untangled from the private revenue streams of adaptive accumulation, will not come to be without a Democratic administration and unified Congressional caucus willing to fight to an unprecedented extent. Even in this scenario, the number of institutional and conflictual political hurdles to be overcome are formidable. As an initial step towards a more efficacious and just public policy, this work has sought to establish a more realistic understanding of the peculiarity of US neoliberalism, with an eye to a better future for all Americans.

References

Abelson, R. (2017) 'No "Death Spiral": Insurers May Soon Profit From Obamacare Plans, Analysis Finds', *The New York Times*, 8 April. Available at: https://www.nytimes.com/2017/04/07/health/insurers-stem-losses-and-may-soon-profit-from-obamacare-plans.html (Accessed: 9 April 2019).

ADC (2019) *Military-Utilities Privatization Group Launches Utilities Advocacy Organization*. Association of Defense Communities. Available at: https://defensecommunities.org/2019/05/military-utilities-privatization-group-launches-utilities-advocacy-organization/ (Accessed: 20 June 2021).

Ahmed, H. (2019) *How Private Prisons Are Profiting Under the Trump Administration*. Center for American Progress. Available at: https://www.americanprogress.org/issues/democracy/reports/2019/08/30/473966/private-prisons-profiting-trump-administration/ (Accessed: 9 June 2020).

Albo, G. (2005) 'Contesting the "New Capitalism"', in Coates, D. (ed.) *Varieties of Capitalism, Varieties of Approaches*. London: Palgrave Macmillan UK, pp. 63–82. doi: 10.1057/9780230522725_4.

Aleaziz, H. (2019) 'More Than 52,000 People Are Now Being Detained By ICE, An Apparent All-Time High', *BuzzFeed News*, 20 May. Available at: https://www.buzzfeednews.com/article/hamedaleaziz/ice-detention-record-immigrants-border (Accessed: 4 May 2021).

Allen, H. *et al.* (2021) 'Comparison of Utilization, Costs, and Quality of Medicaid vs Subsidized Private Health Insurance for Low-Income Adults', *JAMA network open*, 4(1), p. e2032669. doi: 10.1001/jamanetworkopen.2020.32669.

Altman, D. (2020) 'Even supporters may not understand Medicare for All', *Axios*, 2 March. Available at: https://www.axios.com/bernie-sanders-supporters-medicare-for-all-44b8e5bd-45b6-4a91-bcb9-856265b48706.html (Accessed: 2 February 2021).

American Hospital Association (2018) 'Brief as Amici Curiae Opposing Plaintiffs, Texas v. Azar, No. 4:18-cv-00167-O, Doc 123'.

America's Health Insurance Plans *et al.* (2017) 'Letter to Congressional Leadership'. Available at: https://www.ahip.org/wp-content/uploads/2017/11/IM-Coalition-Letter-11_14_2017.pdf (Accessed: 15 June 2019).

America's Health Insurance Plans (2018) 'Brief as Amici Curiae Opposing Plaintiffs, Texas v. Azar, No. 4:18-cv-00167-O, Doc 106–1'.

America's Health Insurance Plans and Blue Cross/Blue Shield (2020) 'Letter to Mitch McConnel, Nancy Pelosi, Chuck Shumer, and Kevin McCarthy'. Available at: https://www.ahip.org/wp-content/uploads/AHIP-BCBSA-Leg-Rec-12.3.20.pdf (Accessed: 8 January 2021).

Archuleta, B. J. (2016) 'Rediscovering Defense Policy: A Public Policy Call to Arms: Rediscovering Defense Policy', *Policy Studies Journal*, 44(S1), pp. S50–S69. doi: 10.1111/psj.12157.

Baker, B. and Miron, G. (2015) 'The business of charter schooling: Understanding the policies that charter operators use for financial benefit.'

Ball, M. (2014) 'The Privatization Backlash', *The Atlantic*, 23 April. Available at: www.theatlantic.com/politics/archive/2014/04/city-state-governments-privatization-contracting-backlash/361016/ (Accessed: 4 July 2017).

Baltodano, M. P. (2017) 'The power brokers of neoliberalism: Philanthrocapitalists and public education', *Policy Futures in Education*, 15(2), pp. 141–156. doi: 10.1177/1478210316652008.

Bauer, S. (2018) 'America's Shocking History of Private Prisons', *Time*, 25 September. Available at: https://time.com/5405158/the-true-history-of-americas-private-prison-industry/ (Accessed: 4 June 2019).

Béland, D. and Waddan, A. (2010) 'The politics of social policy change: lessons of the Clinton and Bush presidencies', *Policy & Politics*, 38, pp. 217–233. doi: 10.1332/030557310X488448.

Berkowitz, E. D. (2010) 'The Scenic Road to Nowhere: Reflections on the History of National Health Insurance in the United States', *The Forum*, 8(1). doi: 10.2202/1540–8884.1350.

Berkowitz, E. D. (2017) 'Getting to the Affordable Care Act', *Journal of Policy History*, 29(4), pp. 519–542. doi: 10.1017/S0898030617000252.

Binelli, M. (2017) 'Michigan Gambled on Charter Schools. Its Children Lost.', *The New York Times*, 5 September. Available at: https://www.nytimes.com/2017/09/05/magazine/michigan-gambled-on-charter-schools-its-children-lost.html (Accessed: 3 January 2020).

Blakely, C. R. (2004) 'Private and Public Sector Prisons: A Comparison of Select Characteristics | Office of Justice Programs', *Federal Probation*, 68(1), pp. 27–31.

Book, R. (2013) *Medicare Advantage Cuts in the Affordable Care Act: March 2013 Update.* American Action Forum. Available at: https://www.americanactionforum.org/insight/medicare-advantage-cuts-in-the-affordable-care-act-march-2013-update/ (Accessed: 4 November 2019).

Bradner, K. *et al.* (2020) *More Work to Do: Analysis of Probation and Parole in the United States, 2017–2018.* Research Brief. Columbia University Justice Lab: Columbia University. Available at: https://academiccommons.columbia.edu/doi/10.7916/d8-hjyq-fg65 (Accessed: 3 January 2021).

Brenner, R. (2006) 'What Is, and What Is Not, Imperialism?', *Historical Materialism*, 14(4), pp. 79–105. doi: 10.1163/156920606778982464.

Britzky, H. (2019) 'Army IG report paints a bleak picture of military housing', *Task & Purpose*, 5 September. Available at: https://taskandpurpose.com/news/army-inspector-general-housing/ (Accessed: 6 January 2020).

Britzky, H. (2020) 'Here's why the "Tenant Bill of Rights" leaves out 3 critical issues important to military families, according to DoD', *Task & Purpose*, 9 March. Available at: https://taskandpurpose.com/news/privatized-housing-lenders-tenant-bill-rights/ (Accessed: 30 June 2020).

Brown, J. *et al.* (2014) 'How Does Risk Selection Respond to Risk Adjustment? New Evidence from the Medicare Advantage Program', *The American Economic Review*, 104(10), pp. 3335–3364. doi: 10.1257/aer.104.10.3335.

Bulkley, K. E. (2011) 'Charter Schools Taking a Closer Look', *Kappa Delta Pi Record*, 47(3), pp. 110–115. doi: 10.1080/00228958.2011.10516573.

Bulkley, K. E. and Burch, P. (2011) 'The Changing Nature of Private Engagement in Public Education: For-Profit and Nonprofit Organizations and Educational Reform', *Peabody Journal of Education*, 86(3), pp. 236–251. doi: 10.1080/0161956X.2011.578963.

Burkhardt, B. (2019a) 'Does the public sector respond to private competition? An analysis of privatization and prison performance', *Journal of Crime and Justice*, 42(2), pp. 201–220. doi: 10.1080/0735648X.2018.1497524.

Burkhardt, B. (2019b) 'The politics of correctional privatization in the United States', *Criminology & Public Policy*, 18(2), pp. 401–418. doi: 10.1111/1745–9133.12431.

Burris, C. and Bryant, J. (2019) *Asleep at the Wheel: How the Federal Charter Schools Program Recklessly Takes Taxpayers and Students for a Ride*. New York: Network for Public Education. Available at: https://networkforpubliceducation.org/asleepatthewheel/ (Accessed: 20 January 2020).

Cancian, M. F. (2019) *US Military Forces in 2020: SOF, Civilians, Contractors and Nukes*. Center for Strategic & International Studies (CSIS). Available at: https://www.csis.org/analysis/us-military-forces-fy-2020-sof-civilians-contractors-and-nukes (Accessed: 6 June 2020).

Carr, P. and Porfilio, B. (2011) 'The Obama Education Files: Is There Hope to Stop the Neoliberal Agenda in Education?', *Journal of Inquiry and Action in Education*, 4(1), pp. 1–30.

Carson, E. A. (2020) 'Prisoners in 2019'. Bureau of Justice Statistics, Bulletin. Available at: bjs.gov/content/pub/pdf/p19.pdf (Accessed: 3 November 2020).

Center for Responsive Ethics (no date) *For-profit Prisons*. Available at: opensecrets.org/industries./indus.php?cycle=2020&ind=G7000 (Accessed: 8 February 2021).

Charest, B. C. (2017) 'The Way It's Going: Neoliberal Reforms and the Colonization of the American School', in Loveless, D. *et al.* (eds) *Deconstructing the Education-Industrial Complex in the Digital Age:* Hershey, PA: IGI Global (Advances in Educational Marketing, Administration, and Leadership), pp. 1–23. doi: 10.4018/978-1-5225-2101-3.

Cheliotis, L. K. (2013) 'Neoliberal capitalism and middle-class punitiveness: Bringing Erich Fromm's "materialistic psychoanalysis" to penology', *Punishment & Society*, 15(3), pp. 247–273. doi: 10.1177/1462474513483692.

Cho, E. (2020) *The Trump Administration Weakens Standards for ICE Detention Facilities*. Common Dreams. Available at: https://www.commondreams.org/views/2020/01/16/trump-administration-weakens-standards-ice-detention-facilities (Accessed: 6 November 2020).

Coates, D. (2014) 'The UK: Less a liberal market economy, more a post-imperial one', *Capital & Class*, 38(1), pp. 171–182. doi: 10.1177/0309816813514816.

Cohen, D. and Lizotte, C. (2015) 'Teaching the market: fostering consent to education markets in the United States', *Environment and Planning A: Economy and Space*, 47(9), pp. 1824–1841. doi: 10.1068/a130273p.

Cohen, M. (2015) 'How for-profit prisons have become the biggest lobby no one is talking about', *Washington Post*, 28 April. Available at: https://www.washingtonpost.com/posteverything/wp/2015/04/28/how-for-profit-prisons-have-become-the-biggest-lobby-no-one-is-talking-about/ (Accessed: 3 January 2020).

Collingwood, L., Morin, J. L. and El-Khatib, S. O. (2018) 'Expanding Carceral Markets: Detention Facilities, ICE Contracts, and the Financial Interests of Punitive Immigration Policy', *Race and Social Problems*, 10(4), pp. 275–292. doi: 10.1007/s12552–018–9241–5.

Commission on Wartime Contracting in Iraq and Afghanistan (2011) 'Transforming wartime contracting: controlling costs, reducing risks: final report to Congress: findings and recommendations for legislative and policy changes'. Available at: https://catalog.library.vanderbilt.edu/discovery/fulldisplay/alma991037752669703276/01VAN_INST:vanui (Accessed: 20 June 2019).

Conca, J. (2020) 'The Feds Try Yet Again To Sell Off BPA And TVA', *Forbes*, 18 February. Available at: https://www.forbes.com/sites/jamesconca/2020/02/18/the-feds-try-yet-again-to-sell-off-bpa-and-tva/ (Accessed: 20 June 2018).

Conger, J. (2018) *An Overview of the DOD Installations Enterprise*. The Heritage Foundation. Available at: https://www.heritage.org/military-strength-topical-essays/2019-essays/over view-the-dod-installations-enterprise (Accessed: 3 March 2109).

Correll, J. T. (2011) 'Origins of the Total Force', *Air Force Magazine*, 1 February. Available at: https://www.airforcemag.com/article/0211force/ (Accessed: 20 June 2020).

Cox, C. and Krutika, A. (2021) *COVID-19 Pandemic-Related Excess Mortality and Potential Years of Life Lost in the U.S. and Peer Countries*. The Kaiser Family Foundation. Available at: https://www.kff.org/coronavirus-covid-19/issue-brief/covid-19-pandemic-related-ex cess-mortality-and-potential-years-of-life-lost-in-the-u-s-and-peer-countries/ (Accessed: 1 June 2021).

Crystal, S. (2003) 'Groundhog Day: The Endless Debate Over Medicare "Reform"', *Public Policy & Aging Report*, 13(4), pp. 7–10. doi: 10.1093/ppar/13.4.7.

Daniels, J. (2017) 'Base closings "hot potato" issue again as Pentagon insists new round could save tens of billions', *CNBC*, 19 July. Available at: https://www.cnbc.com/2017/07/14/base-closings-hot-potato-issue-again-as-pentagon-insists-new-round-could-save-tens-of-billions.html (Accessed: 5 February 2020).

Darder, A. (2015) 'Forward', in Sturges, K. M. (ed.) *Neoliberalizing educational reform: America's quest for profitable market-colonies and the undoing of public good*. Rotterdam: Sense Publishers, p. xi.

Davis, A. (1998) 'Masked Racism: Reflections on the Prison Industrial Complex', *Colorlines: Race, Culture, Action*, 10 September, pp. 11–12.

De Giorgi, A. (2007) 'Toward a political economy of post-Fordist punishment', *Critical Criminology*, 15(3), pp. 243–265. doi: 10.1007/s10612–007–9029–1.

Demko, P. and Cancryn, A. (2018) 'Trump's new health insurance rules expected to hurt Obamacare', *Politico*, 19 June. Available at: https://politi.co/2K2M07U (Accessed: 3 February 2020).

Donziger, S. (1996) 'The Prison-Industrial Complex', *Washington Post*, 17 March. Available at: https://www.washingtonpost.com/archive/opinions/1996/03/17/the-prison-industrial-complex/6cd7b498-ad9b-4cf2-8ccb-a1b605e25fea/ (Accessed: 5 April 2020).

Eisen, L.-B. (2019) *Inside private prisons: an American dilemma in the age of mass incarceration*. Columbia.

Eisenberg, A. K. (2016) 'Incarceration Incentives in the Decarceration Era', *SSRN Electronic Journal*, 69, pp. 71–139. doi: 10.2139/ssrn.2719013.

Ellison, A. (2015) 'CMS finalizes 2016 Medicare Advantage payment rates: 10 things to know', *Becker's Hospital Review*, 7 April. Available at: https://www.beckershospitalreview.com/fi nance/cms-finalizes-2016-medicare-advantage-payment-rates-10-things-to-know.html (Accessed: 21 June 2020).

Ellison, A. (2016) 'CMS finalizes 2017 Medicare Advantage rates: 8 things to know', *Becker's Hospital Review*, 5 April. Available at: https://www.beckershospitalreview.com/finance/cms-finalizes-2017-medicare-advantage-rates-8-things-to-know.html (Accessed: 21 June 2020).

Evers-Hillstrom, K. (2021) *Healthcare interests, restaurants among COVID relief bill winners.* OpenSecrets News. Available at: https://www.opensecrets.org/news/2021/03/covid-relief-bill-winners/ (Accessed: 20 June 2020).

Fallows, J. (2002) 'The Military-Industrial Complex', *Foreign Policy*, (133), pp. 46–48. doi: 10.2307/3183556.

Ferguson, N. (2005) *Colossus: the rise and fall of the American empire.* New York: Penguin Books.

Frankel, A. and Pitter, L. (2020) *Revoked: how probation and parole feed mass incarceration in the United States.* Background Report. Human Rights Watch/American Civil Liberites Union. Available at: https://www.hrw.org/sites/default/files/media_2020/07/us_supervision0720_web_1.pdf (Accessed: 4 March 2021).

Fraser, N. (2019) *The old is dying and the new cannot be born: from progressive neoliberalism to Trump and beyond.* New York: Verso.

Freedman, L. (1998) 'Introduction', *The Adelphi Papers*, 38(318), pp. 5–10. doi: 10.1080/05679329808449499.

Gaes, G. G. (2019) 'Current status of prison privatization research on American prisons and jails', *Criminology & Public Policy*, 18(2), pp. 269–293. doi: 10.1111/1745–9133.12428.

Gaffney, A., Himmelstein, D. U. and Woolhandler, S. (2021) 'Congressional Budget Office Scores Medicare-For-All: Universal Coverage For Less Spending', *Health Affairs Blog*, 16 February. Available at: https://www.healthaffairs.org/do/10.1377/hblog20210210.190243/full/ (Accessed: 21 April 2021).

Gagnon, M.-A. (2015) 'US Medicare Part D drug prices needlessly high', *PharmacoEconomics & Outcomes News*, 734(1), pp. 28–28. doi: 10.1007/s40274–015–2365–6.

Gautreaux, M. T. (2015) 'Neoliberal education reform's mouthpiece: Analyzing Education Week's discourse on Teach for America', *Critical Education*, 6(11), pp. 1–17. doi: 10.14288/CE.V6I11.185228.

Gerstenberger, H. (2011) 'The Historical Constitution of the Political Forms of Capitalism', *Antipode*, 43(1), pp. 60–86. doi: 10.1111/j.1467–8330.2010.00811.x.

Geyman, J. (2018) 'Crisis in U.S. Health Care: Corporate Power Still Blocks Reform', *International Journal of Health Services: Planning, Administration, Evaluation*, 48(1), pp. 5–27. doi: 10.1177/0020731417729654.

Giaimo, S. and Manow, P. (1999) 'Adapting the Welfare State: The Case of Health Care Reform in Britain, Germany, and the United States', *Comparative Political Studies*, 32(8), pp. 967–1000. doi: 10.1177/0010414099032008003.

Giroux, H. A. and Saltman, K. (2009) 'Obama's Betrayal of Public Education? Arne Duncan and the Corporate Model of Schooling', *Cultural Studies ↔ Critical Methodologies*, 9(6), pp. 772–779. doi: 10.1177/1532708609348575.

Gleason, P. *et al.* (2010) *The Evaluation of Charter School Impacts.* Washington, DC: National Center for Education Evaluation and Regional Assistance, Institute of Education Sciences, U.S. Department of Education. Available at: https://ies.ed.gov/ncee/pubs/20104029/pdf/20104029.pdf (Accessed: 3 February 2019).

Godfrey, M. C. *et al.* (2012) *A history of the U.S. Army's Residential Communities Initiative, 1995–2010: privatizing military family housing.* Washington, D.C.: U.S. G.P.O.

Goodin, R. E. (2003) 'Choose Your Capitalism?', *Comparative European Politics*, 1(2), pp. 203–213. doi: 10.1057/palgrave.cep.6110009.

Goodland, M. (2020) 'Senate Judiciary Committee makes sweeping changes to private prison bill', *Colorado Springs Gazette*, 13 February. Available at: https://gazette.com/news/sen ate-judiciary-committee-makes-sweeping-changes-to-private-prison-bill/article_5dabc4bb-1cff-5c99-9d1a-8385f31f0ad6.html (Accessed: 4 March 2021).

Gramlich, J. (2020) *How border apprehensions, ICE arrests and deportations have changed under Trump*. Pew Research Center. Available at: https://www.pewresearch.org/fact-tank/2020/03/02/how-border-apprehensions-ice-arrests-and-deportations-have-changed-under-trump/ (Accessed: 1 March 2021).

Greene, P. (2020) 'DeVos Makes New Charter School Grants From Troubled Fund', *Forbes*, 11 April. Available at: https://www.forbes.com/sites/petergreene/2020/04/11/devos-makes-new-charter-school-grants-from-troubled-fund/ (Accessed: 4 May 2021).

Greer, J. M. (2014) *Decline and fall: the end of empire and the future of democracy in 21st century America*. Gabriola, BC: New Society Publishers.

Haberkorn, J. (2018) 'Spending deals signal end of unpopular Obamacare cost checks', *Politico*, 19 February. Available at: http://politi.co/2EDthtw (Accessed: 21 June 2019).

Haberkorn, J. and Norman, B. (2013) 'CMS reverses course on cuts', *Politico*, 3 April. Available at: https://www.politico.com/story/2013/04/insurance-medicare-advantage-cuts-health-care-089569 (Accessed: 21 May 2019).

Hacker, J. (2002) *The Divided Welfare State: The Battle over Public and Private Social Benefits in the United States*. 1st edn. Cambridge University Press. doi: 10.1017/CBO9780511817298.

Hacker, J. (2004) 'Privatizing Risk Without Privatizing the Welfare State: The Hidden Politics of Social Policy Retrenchment in the United States', *American Political Science Review*, 98(2), pp. 243–260. doi: 10.1017/S0003055404001121.

Hacker, J. (2010) 'The Road to Somewhere: Why Health Reform Happened: Or Why Political Scientists Who Write about Public Policy Shouldn't Assume They Know How to Shape It', *Perspectives on Politics*, 8(3), pp. 861–876. doi: 10.1017/S1537592710002021.

Hanson, M. (no date) 'U.S. Public Education Spending Statistics'. EducationData. Available at: https://educationdata.org/public-education-spending-statistics (Accessed: 6 March 2020).

Harris, G. (2003) 'Cheap Drugs From Canada: Another Political Hot Potato – The New York Times', *New York Times*, 23 October. Available at: https://www.nytimes.com/2003/10/23/business/cheap-drugs-from-canada-another-political-hot-potato.html (Accessed: 21 July 2020).

Harvey, D. (2005) *The new imperialism*. Oxford ; New York: Oxford University Press.

Harvey, D. (2011) *A brief history of neoliberalism*. Oxford: Oxford Univ. Press.

Hayford, T. B. and Burns, A. L. (2018) 'Medicare Advantage Enrollment and Beneficiary Risk Scores: Difference-in-Differences Analyses Show Increases for All Enrollees On Account of Market-Wide Changes', *Inquiry: A Journal of Medical Care Organization, Provision and Financing*, 55, pp. 1–11. doi: 10.1177/0046958018788640.

Hellmann, J. (2017) 'Insurer trade group blasts latest ObamaCare repeal bill', *The Hill*, 20 September. Available at: https://thehill.com/policy/healthcare/351592-insurer-trade-group-opposes-latest-obamacare-repeal-bill (Accessed: 21 January 2020).

Henwood, D. (2011) 'Before and After the Crisis: Wall Street Lives On', in Panitch, L., Albo, G., and Chibber, V. (eds) *Socialist Register 2011: The Crisis This Time*. London: Merlin, pp. 83–97.

Herbert, B. (2014) 'The Plot Against Public Education: How millionaires and billionaires are ruining our schools.', *Politico*, 6 October. Available at: https://www.politico.com/mag azine/story/2014/10/the-plot-against-public-education-111630 (Accessed: 22 June 2018).

Himmelstein, D. U. *et al.* (2018) 'The U.S. Health Care Crisis Continues: A Data Snapshot', *International Journal of Health Services: Planning, Administration, Evaluation*, 48(1), pp. 28–41. doi: 10.1177/0020731417741779.

Hoadley, J. F., Cubanski, J. and Neuman, P. (2015) 'Medicare's Part D Drug Benefit At 10 Years: Firmly Established But Still Evolving', *Health Affairs*, 34(10), pp. 1682–1687. doi: 10.1377/hlthaff.2015.0927.

Hoadley, J. F., Cubanski, J. and Neuman, T. (2016) *Medicare Part D in 2016 and Trends over Time*. The Kaiser Family Foundation. Available at: https://www.kff.org/medicare/report/medicare-part-d-in-2016-and-trends-over-time/ (Accessed: 21 June 2020).

Hoffman, B. (2010) 'The Challenge of Universal Healthcare', in Banaszak-Holl, J., Levitsky, S., and Zald, M. (eds) *Social Movements and the Transformation of American Health Care*. Oxford: Oxford University Press. doi: 10.1093/acprof:oso/9780195388299.001.0001.

Hollingsworth, R. (1997) 'The Institutional Embeddedness of American Capitalism', in Crouch, C. and Streeck, W. (eds) *Political Economy of Modern Capitalism: Mapping Convergence and Diversity*. London: Sage, pp. 133–47.

Howell, C. (2003) 'Varieties of Capitalism: And Then There Was One?', *Comparative Politics*, 36(1), pp. 103–24. doi: 10.2307/4150162.

Howley, Caitlin and Howley, Craig (2015) 'Farming the Poor', in Sturges, K. M. (ed.) *Neoliberalizing Educational Reform*. Rotterdam: SensePublishers, pp. 23–51. doi: 10.1007/978-94-6209-977-7_2.

In the Public Interest (2013) *Criminal: How Lockup Quotas and 'Low-Crime Taxes' Guarantee Profits for Private Prison Corporations*. Available at: https://www.inthepublicinterest.org/criminal-how-lockup-quotas-and-low-crime-taxes-guarantee-profits-for-private-prison-cor porations/ (Accessed: 20 October 2020).

Ingraham, C. (2015) 'The U.S. has more jails than colleges. Here's a map of where those prisoners live.', *Washington Post*, 6 January. Available at: https://www.washingtonpost.com/news/wonk/wp/2015/01/06/the-u-s-has-more-jails-than-colleges-heres-a-map-of-where-those-prisoners-live/ (Accessed: 4 March 2018).

Isenberg, D. (2011) *Security Contractors and U.S. Defense: Lessons Learned from Iraq and Afghanistan*. Cato Institute. Available at: https://www.cato.org/publications/com mentary/security-contractors-us-defense-lessons-learned-iraq-afghanistan (Accessed: 20 June 2020).

Jaenicke, D. and Waddan, A. (2006) 'President Bush and Social Policy: The Strange Case of the Medicare Prescription Drug Benefit', *Political Science Quarterly*, 121(2), pp. 217–240.

Jankov, P. and Caref, C. (2017) 'Segregation and Inequality in Chicago Public Schools, Transformed and Intensified under Corporate Education Reform', *Education Policy Analysis Archives*, 25(56), pp. 1–30.

Jennings, K. (2015) 'Nonprofit insurers lose on Medicare under new Obamacare rules', *Politico*, 19 August. Available at: https://www.politico.com/states/new-york/albany/story/2015/08/nonprofit-insurers-lose-on-medicare-under-new-obamacare-rules-024829 (Accessed: 4 March 2018).

Jenson, J. and Mérand, F. (2010) 'Sociology, institutionalism and the European Union', *Comparative European Politics*, 8(1), pp. 74–92. doi: 10.1057/cep.2010.5.

Jessop, B. (2001) 'Institutional Re(turns) and the Strategic – Relational Approach', *Environment and Planning A: Economy and Space*, 33(7), pp. 1213–1235. doi: 10.1068/a32183.

Jessop, B. (2008) 'Dialogue of the Deaf: Some Reflections on the Poulantzas-Miliband Debate', in Wetherly, P., Barrow, C. W., and Burnham, P. (eds) *Class, Power and the State in Capitalist Society*. London: Palgrave Macmillan, pp. 132–157. doi: 10.1057/9780230592704_7.

Jing, Y. (2010) 'Prison privatization: a perspective on core governmental functions', *Crime, Law and Social Change*, 54(3–4), pp. 263–278. doi: 10.1007/s10611–010–9254–5.

Keith, K. (2018) 'All Parties In Texas v. Azar Ask For Appeal To 5th Circuit', *Health Affairs Blog*, 22 December. Available at: https://www.healthaffairs.org/do/10.1377/hblog20181221.897066/full/ (Accessed: 21 June 2020).

Keith, K. (2019) 'ACA Provisions In New Budget Bill', *Health Affairs Blog*, 20 December. Available at: https://www.healthaffairs.org/do/10.1377/hblog20191220.115975/full/ (Accessed: 21 June 2020).

Kelly, A. S. (2016) 'Boutique to Booming: Medicare Managed Care and the Private Path to Policy Change', *Journal of Health Politics, Policy and Law*, 41(3), pp. 315–354. doi: 10.1215/03616878–3523934.

Knafo, S. and Teschke, B. (2020) 'Political Marxism and the Rules of Reproduction of Capitalism: A Historicist Critique', *Historical Materialism*, 15(2), pp. 75–104. doi: 10.1163/1569206X-00001441.

Konings, M. (2012) 'Imagined Double Movements: Progressive Thought and the Specter of Neoliberal Populism', *Globalizations*, 9(4), pp. 609–622. doi: 10.1080/14747731.2012.699939.

Kronick, R. (2017) 'Projected Coding Intensity In Medicare Advantage Could Increase Medicare Spending By $200 Billion Over Ten Years', *Health Affairs*, 36(2), pp. 320–327. doi: 10.1377/hlthaff.2016.0768.

Ladipo, D. (2001) 'The rise of America's prison-industrial complex', *New Left review*, 7, pp. 109–123.

Langman, L. (2012) 'Cycles of Contention: The Rise and Fall of the Tea Party', *Critical Sociology*, 38(4), pp. 469–494. doi: 10.1177/0896920511430865.

Layton, L. (2014) 'How Bill Gates pulled off the swift Common Core revolution', *Washington Post*, 7 June. Available at: https://www.washingtonpost.com/politics/how-bill-gates-pulled-off-the-swift-common-core-revolution/2014/06/07/a830e32e-ec34-11e3-9f5c-9075d5508f0a_story.html (Accessed: 4 March 2020).

Leander, A. (2005) 'The Market for Force and Public Security: The Destabilizing Consequences of Private Military Companies', *Journal of Peace Research*, 42(5), pp. 605–622.

Levitt, L., Cox, C. and Claxton, G. (2017) *The Effects of Ending the Affordable Care Act's Cost-Sharing Reduction Payments*. The Kaiser Family Foundation. Available at: https://www.kff.org/health-reform/issue-brief/the-effects-of-ending-the-affordable-care-acts-cost-sharing-reduction-payments/ (Accessed: 1 March 2019).

Lichtenstein, N. (2017) 'Who Killed Obamacare?', *Dissent*, 64(2), pp. 26–33.

Loeppky, R. (2010) 'Certain Wealth: accumulation in the health industry', in Panitch, L. and Leys, C. (eds) *Socialist Register 2010: Morbid Symptoms*. London: Merlin, pp. 59–83.

Loeppky, R. (2014) *Accumulation and constraint: biomedical development and advanced industrial health*. Halifax: Fernwood Publishing.

Loeppky, R. (2019) 'The Real Meaning of "Managed Care": Adaptive Accumulation and U.S. Health Care', *International Journal of Health Services*, 49(4), pp. 733–753. doi: 10.1177/0020731419863651.

Looney, A. and Turner, N. (2018) *Work and opportunity before and after incarceration*. The Brookings Institution. Available at: https://www.brookings.edu/wp-content/uploads/2018/03/es_20180314_looneyincarceration_final.pdf (Accessed: 4 May 2021).

Losen, D. J. *et al.* (2016) *Charter Schools, Civil Rights and School Discipline: A Comprehensive Review*. UCLA: The Civil Rights Project / Proyecto Derechos Civiles. Available at: https://escholarship.org/uc/item/65x5j31h (Accessed: 4 March 2019).

Luthi, S. (2021) 'The Supreme Court saved Obamacare. Now supporters want Biden to fix the law.', *Politico*, 24 June. Available at: https://www.politico.com/news/2021/06/24/supreme-court-obamacare-law-495755 (Accessed: 12 July 2021).

Martin, A. B. *et al.* (2021) 'National Health Care Spending In 2019: Steady Growth For The Fourth Consecutive Year: Study examines national health care spending for 2019.', *Health Affairs*, 40(1), pp. 14–24. doi: 10.1377/hlthaff.2020.02022.

McFate, S. (2016) 'America's Addiction to Mercenaries', *The Atlantic*, 12 August. Available at: https://www.theatlantic.com/international/archive/2016/08/iraq-afghanistan-contractor-pentagon-obama/495731/ (Accessed: 20 June 2019).

McGuire, T. G., Newhouse, J. P. and Sinaiko, A. D. (2011) 'An economic history of Medicare part C', *The Milbank Quarterly*, 89(2), pp. 289–332. doi: 10.1111/j.1468-0009.2011.00629.x.

Michels, J. (2021) 'Winning Medicare for All Would Have Massive Implications Beyond Health Care', *Jacobin Magazine*, 31 March. Available at: https://jacobinmag.com/2021/03/medicare-for-all-citizens-guide-health-care (Accessed: 19 June 2021).

Miliband, R. (1970) 'The capitalist state: reply to Nicos Poulantzas', *New Left Review*, 59(1), pp. 53–60.

Millman, J. (2014) 'Obama administration reverses proposed cut to Medicare plans', *Washington Post*, 7 April. Available at: https://www.washingtonpost.com/news/wonk/wp/2014/04/07/obama-administration-reverses-proposed-cut-to-medicare-plans/ (Accessed: 1 June 2017).

Mitchell, J. L. and Butz, A. M. (2019) 'Social Control Meets New Public Management: Examining the Diffusion of State Prison Privatization, 1979-2010', *Politics & Policy*, 47(3), pp. 506–544. doi: 10.1111/polp.12309.

Moreno, K. and Price, B. E. (2018) 'All in the Name of National Security: The Profiting from Xenophobia by Private Corporations in the Trump Era', in Bures, O. and Carrapico, H. (eds) *Security Privatization*. Cham: Springer International Publishing, pp. 143–172. doi: 10.1007/978-3-319-63010-6_7.

Morse, S. (2017) 'CMS gives bigger increase to Medicare Advantage payment rates for 2018', *Healthcare Finance News*, 3 April. Available at: https://www.healthcarefinancenews.com/news/cms-gives-bigger-increase-medicare-advantage-payment-rates-2018 (Accessed: 7 March 2019).

National Center for Education Statistics (2018) 'Number and enrollment of public elementary and secondary schools, by school level, type, and charter, magnet, and virtual status: Selected years, 1990–91 through 2016–17'. Digest of Education Statistics. Available at: https://nces.ed.gov/programs/digest/d18/tables/dt18_216.20.asp?current=yes (Accessed: 7 March 2019).

National Center for Education Statistics (2019) *The Condition of Education 2019*. NCES 2019–144. Available at: nces.ed.gov/pubs2019/2019144.pdf (Accessed: 4 May 2020).

Nellis, A. (2016) *The Color of Justice: Racial and Ethnic Disparity in State Prisons*. The Sentencing Project. Available at: file:///Users/rodney/Downloads/The-Color-of-Justice-Racial-and-Ethnic-Disparity-in-State-Prisons.pdf (Accessed: 5 May 2021).

Newhouse, J. P. *et al.* (2015) 'How Much Favouable Selection is Left in Medicare Advantage?', *American Journal of Health Economics*, 1(1), pp. 1–26. doi: 10.1162/AJHE_a_00001.

Norman, B. (2014) 'Ad blitz to preempt Medicare cuts', *Politico*, 14 January. Available at: https://www.politico.com/story/2014/01/insurance-industry-ads-medicare-cuts-102158 (Accessed: 21 June 2019).

Norman, B. and Karli-Smith, S. (2016) 'The one that got away: Obamacare and the drug industry', *Politico*, 13 July. Available at: https://www.politico.com/story/2016/07/obama care-prescription-drugs-pharma-225444 (Accessed: 5 June 2017).

Oberlander, J. (2007) 'Through the Looking Glass: The Politics of the Medicare Prescription Drug, Improvement, and Modernization Act', *Journal of Health Politics, Policy and Law*, 32(2), pp. 187–219. doi: 10.1215/03616878–2006–036.

Oberlander, J. (2014) 'Voucherizing Medicare', *Journal of Health Politics, Policy and Law*, 39(2), pp. 467–482. doi: 10.1215/03616878–2416348.

Oberlander, J. (2016) 'Implementing the Affordable Care Act: The Promise and Limits of Health Care Reform', *Journal of Health Politics, Policy and Law*, 41(4), pp. 803–826. doi: 10.1215/03616878–3620953.

OECD (2019) *Health at a Glance 2019: OECD Indicators*. OECD (Health at a Glance). doi: 10.1787/4dd50c09-en.

OECD (2021a) 'Health spending'. OECD. doi: 10.1787/8643de7e-en.

OECD (2021b) 'Pharmaceutical spending'. OECD. doi: 10.1787/998febf6-en.

O'Hanlon, M. (1998) 'Can High Technology Bring U. S. Troops Home?', *Foreign Policy*, (113), pp. 72–86. doi: 10.2307/1149234.

Olson, J. (2008) 'Whiteness and the Polarization of American Politics', *Political Research Quarterly*, 61(4), pp. 704–718.

Osborn, J. and Beier, D. (2017) '"Repealing And Replacing" Obamacare: Whatever You Do, Preserve Medicare Part D And Fill The Donut Hole', *Forbes*, 17 January. Available at: https://www.forbes.com/sites/johnosborn/2017/01/13/repealing-replacing-obamacare-whatever-you-do-preserve-medicare-part-d-and-fill-the-donut-hole/ (Accessed: 21 June 2020).

Panitch, L. (1994) 'Globalization and the State', in Panitch, L. and Miliband, R. (eds) *Socialist Register 1994: Between Globalism and Nationalism*. London: Merlin, pp. 60–93.

Panitch, L. (1999) 'The Impoverishment of State Theory', *Socialism and Democracy*, 13(2), pp. 19–35. doi: 10.1080/08854309908428242.

Pauly, M. (2020) 'How a private prison company's defamation suit against one of its critics backfired', *Mother Jones*, 11 December. Available at: https://www.motherjones.com/crime-justice/2020/12/corecivic-defamation-lawsuit-family-separation-simon/ (Accessed: 5 May 2021).

Pear, R. (2017) 'Insurers Come Out Swinging Against New Republican Health Care Bill', *The New York Times*, 20 September. Available at: https://www.nytimes.com/2017/09/20/us/politics/insurers-oppose-obamacare-repeal.html (Accessed: 21 January 2021).

Peet, R. (ed.) (2003) *Unholy trinity: the IMF, World Bank and WTO*. Malaysia ; SIRD, London ; New York: Zed Books.

Pell, M. B. (2019a) 'Special Report: Ex-workers say U.S. military landlord falsified records to get bonuses', *Reuters*, 20 November. Available at: https://cn.reuters.com/article/uk-usa-military-lackland-specialreport-idINKBN1XU1HV (Accessed: 8 February 2020).

Pell, M. B. (2019b) 'Special Report: U.S. Air Force landlord falsified records to boost income: documents', *Reuters*, 18 June. Available at: https://www.reuters.com/investigates/spe cial-report/usa-military-maintenance/ (Accessed: 8 February 2020).

Pell, M. B. and Nelson, D. (2018) 'Special Report: U.S. military's new housing plagued by construction flaws', *Reuters*, 21 December. Available at: https://www.reuters.com/article/us-usa-military-construction-special-rep-idUSKCN1OK153 (Accessed: 9 February 2020).

Petersohn, U. (2014) 'Reframing the anti-mercenary norm: Private military and security companies and mercenarism', *International Journal*, 69(4), pp. 475–493.

Pilon, D. (2015) 'Critical Institutionalism: Recovering the Lost Social Core of Institutionalism', in *Annual Western Social Science Conference. Annual Western Social Science Conference*, Portland.

Porter, S. (2018) *Medicare Advantage Plans to Get 3.4% Pay Increase.* healthleaders. Available at: https://www.healthleadersmedia.com/finance/medicare-advantage-plans-get-34-pay-increase (Accessed: 4 February 2019).

Poulantzas, N. (1969) 'The problem of the capitalist state', *New left review*, 58(1), pp. 67–78.

Raher, S. (2010) 'The Business of Punishing: Impediments to Accountability in the Private Corrections Industry', *Richmond Journal of Law and the Public Interest*, 13(2), pp. 209–249.

Rahman, M. *et al.* (2015) 'High-Cost Patients Had Substantial Rates Of Leaving Medicare Advantage And Joining Traditional Medicare', *Health Affairs*, 34(10), pp. 1675–1681. doi: 10.1377/hlthaff.2015.0272.

Rao, B. and Hellander, I. (2014) 'The widening U.S. health care crisis three years after the passage of "Obamacare"', *International Journal of Health Services: Planning, Administration, Evaluation*, 44(2), pp. 215–232. doi: 10.2190/HS.44.2.b.

Ravitch, D. (2016) 'Opinion | The Common Core Costs Billions and Hurts Students', *The New York Times*, 23 July. Available at: https://www.nytimes.com/2016/07/24/opinion/sunday/the-common-core-costs-billions-and-hurts-students.html (Accessed: 4 March 2020).

Rawls, K. (2013) *Who Is Profiting From Charters? The Big Bucks Behind Charter School Secrecy, Financial Scandal and Corruption.* Alternet.org. Available at: https://www.alter net.org/2013/05/who-profiting-charters-big-bucks-behind-charter-school-secrecy-finan cial-scandal-and/ (Accessed: 20 November 2018).

Rimbach, J. and Koloff, A. (2019) 'How investors and developers use properties to cash in on NJ charter school growth', *New Jersey Record*, 27 March. Available at: https://www.north jersey.com/in-depth/news/watchdog/2019/03/27/how-investors-and-developers-cash-nj-charter-school-growth/2981158002/ (Accessed: 22 June 2020).

Rock, J. (2021) 'The Fight for Health Care for All Is Opening Up in the States', *Jacobin Magazine*, 19 April. Available at: https://jacobinmag.com/2021/04/public-option-health-care-biden-washington-colorado (Accessed: 20 June 2021).

Roy, A. (2012) 'Why Closing Medicare's "Donut Hole" is a Terrible Idea', *Forbes*, 23 May. Available at: https://www.forbes.com/sites/theapothecary/2012/05/23/why-closing-medi cares-donut-hole-is-a-terrible-idea/ (Accessed: 20 June 2020).

Saltman, K. (2009) 'The Rise of Venture Philanthropy and the Ongoing Neoliberal Assault on Public Education: The Eli and Edythe Broad Foundation', *Workplace: A Journal for Academic Labor*, 16, pp. 53–72. doi: 10.14288/WORKPLACE.VOI16.182244.

Saltman, K. J. (2007) 'Schooling in Disaster Capitalism: How the Political Right Is Using Disaster To Privatize Public Schooling', *Teacher Education Quarterly*, 34(2), pp. 131–156.

Saltman, K. J. (2014) 'Neoliberalism and Corporate School Reform: "Failure" and "Creative Destruction"', *Review of Education, Pedagogy, and Cultural Studies*, 36(4), pp. 249–259. doi: 10.1080/10714413.2014.938564.

Saltman, K. J. (2018) *The Swindle of Innovative Educational Finance*. Minneapolis: University of Minnesota Press.

Schept, J. (2013) '"A lockdown facility … with the feel of a small, private college": Liberal politics, jail expansion, and the carceral habitus', *Theoretical Criminology*, 17(1), pp. 71–88. doi: 10.1177/1362480612463113.

Schlosser, E. (1998) 'The Prison-Industrial Complex', *The Atlantic*, 1 December. Available at: https://www.theatlantic.com/magazine/archive/1998/12/the-prison-industrial-complex/304669/ (Accessed: 4 March 2016).

Schnaubelt, C. (2017) *Making BRAC Politically Palatable*. RAND Corporation. Available at: https://www.rand.org/blog/2017/03/making-brac-politically-palatable.html (Accessed: 3 March 2019).

Schwartz, M. and Swain, J. (2011) *Department of Defense Contractors in Afghanistan and Iraq: Background and Analysis*. Congressional Research Service. Available at: https://apps.dtic.mil/sti/citations/ADA585309 (Accessed: 8 February 2019).

Scott, J. (2009) 'The Politics of Venture Philanthropy in Charter School Policy and Advocacy', *Educational Policy*, 23(1), pp. 106–136. doi: 10.1177/0895904808328531.

Scott, J. (2011) 'Market-Driven Education Reform and the Racial Politics of Advocacy', *Peabody Journal of Education*, 86(5), pp. 580–599. doi: 10.1080/0161956X.2011.616445.

Serwer, A. (2019) 'A Crime by Any Name', *The Atlantic*, 3 July. Available at: https://www.theatlantic.com/ideas/archive/2019/07/border-facilities/593239/ (Accessed: 5 January 2020).

Simon, M. (2021) 'What Does Biden's "Ban" On Private Prisons Really Mean?', *Forbes*, 27 January. Available at: https://www.forbes.com/sites/morgansimon/2021/01/27/what-does-bidens-ban-on-private-prisons-really-mean/ (Accessed: 4 May 2021).

Singer, P. W. (2005) 'Outsourcing War', *Foreign Affairs*, 84(2), pp. 119–132. doi: 10.2307/20034280.

Sinha, A. (2017) 'Arbitrary Detention? The Immigration Detention Bed Quota', *Duke Journal of Constitutional Law & Public Policy*, 12(2), pp. 77–121.

SIPRI (2016) *Global arms industry: USA remains dominant despite decline; sales rise in Western Europe and Russia, says SIPRI*. Press Release. Available at: https://www.sipri.org/media/press-release/2016/global-arms-industry-usa-remains-dominant (Accessed: 20 January 2019).

Slater, G. B. (2015) 'Education as recovery: neoliberalism, school reform, and the politics of crisis', *Journal of Education Policy*, 30(1), pp. 1–20. doi: 10.1080/02680939.2014.904930.

Sorensen, T. C. (1990) 'Rethinking National Security', *Foreign Affairs*, 69(3), pp. 1–18. doi: 10.2307/20044397.

Spreen, C. A. and Stark, L. (2014) 'Privatization Nation: How the United States Became the Land of "Edupreneurs"', *Our Schools, Our Selves*, 23(4), pp. 153–175.

Stageman, D. L. (2013) '"These Illegals": Personhood, Profit, and the Political Economy of Punishment in Federal–Local Immigration Enforcement Partnerships', in Brotherton, D. C., Stageman, D. L., and Leyro, S. P. (eds) *Outside Justice*. New York: Springer, pp. 223–245. doi: 10.1007/978-1-4614-6648-2_12.

Starr, P. (2013) *Remedy and reaction: the peculiar American struggle over health care reform*. Revised edition. New Haven: Yale University Press.

Strasser, A.-R. (2012) *Health Care Insurers Spent $100 Million To Defeat Obamacare*. ThinkProgress. Available at: https://archive.thinkprogress.org/health-care-insurers-spent-100-million-to-defeat-obamacare-4ed855719a76/ (Accessed: 21 June 2020).

Strauss, V. (2020) 'The 5 most serious charter school scandals in 2019 – and why they matter', *Washington Post*, 27 January. Available at: https://www.washingtonpost.com/education/2020/01/27/5-most-serious-charter-school-scandals-2019-why-they-matter/ (Accessed: 6 June 2020).

Stuit, D. A. and Smith, T. M. (2012) 'Explaining the gap in charter and traditional public school teacher turnover rates', *Economics of Education Review*, 31(2), pp. 268–279. doi: 10.1016/j.econedurev.2011.09.007.

Sturges, K. M. (2015) 'Educational Reform in the Age of Neoliberalism', in Sturges, K. M. (ed.) *Neoliberalizing Educational Reform*. Rotterdam: SensePublishers, pp. 1–19. doi: 10.1007/978-94-6209-977-7_1.

Swenson, P. and Greer, S. (2002) 'Foul weather friends: big business and health care reform in the 1990s in historical perspective', *Journal of Health Politics, Policy and Law*, 27(4), pp. 605–638. doi: 10.1215/03616878–27–4–605.

Takei, C. (2017) *Private Prison Giant CoreCivic Wants to Corner the Mass Incarceration 'Market' in the States*. American Civil Liberties Union. Available at: https://www.aclu.org/blog/smart-justice/mass-incarceration/private-prison-giant-corecivics-wants-corner-mass (Accessed: 3 November 2020).

The Kaiser Family Foundation (2017) *The Medicare Part D Prescription Drug Benefit*. Available at: kff.org/medicare/fact-sheet/the-medicare-prescription-drug-benefit-fact-sheet (Accessed: 9 March 2019).

The Kaiser Family Foundation (2019) *10 Essential Facts About Medicare and Prescription Drug Spending*. Available at: https://www.kff.org/infographic/10-essential-facts-about-medicare-and-prescription-drug-spending/ (Accessed: 21 March 2020).

The Kaiser Family Foundation (2021) *Marketplace Enrollment, 2014–2021*. Available at: https://www.kff.org/health-reform/state-indicator/marketplace-enrollment/ (Accessed: 21 January 2021).

Thorpe, R. U. (2010) 'The Role of Economic Reliance in Defense Procurement Contracting', *American Politics Research*, 38(4), pp. 636–675. doi: 10.1177/1532673X09337107.

Tuchman Mathews, J. (1989) 'Redefining Security', *Foreign Affairs*, 68(2), pp. 162–177. doi: 10.2307/20043906.

Ujifusa, A. (2020) 'DeVos Grilled Over Education Budget Proposal at Congressional Hearing', *Education Week*, 4 March. Available at: https://www.edweek.org/policy-politics/devos-grilled-over-education-budget-proposal-at-congressional-hearing/2020/03 (Accessed: 6 June 2020).

UPP (2019) *Utilities Privatization System Owners Launch New Group.* Utility Privatization Partners. Available at: http://utilityprivatization.org/utilities-privatization-system-owners-launch-new-group/ (Accessed: 20 June 2019).

US Congress (1996) *National Defense Authorization Act for Fiscal Year 1996, Public Law 104–106, US Statutes at Large 10.*

US Congress (1997) 'National Defense Authorization Act for Fiscal Year 1998, Public Law 105–85, US Statutes at Large 111'.

US Congress (2003) 'Medicare Prescription Drug, Improvement, and Modernization Act of 2003, Public Law 108–173, US Statutes At Large 117'.

US Congress, House (2008) *Private Prison Information Act of 2007 (Part II).* 110th Congress, 2nd Session. Available at: https://www.govinfo.gov/content/pkg/CHRG-110hhrg43153/html/CHRG-110hhrg43153.htm (Accessed: 5 January 2021).

US Congress, House (2019) 'H.R. 5087-Private Prison Information Act of 2019'. 116th Congress, 1st Session. Available at: congress.gov/116/bills/hr5087/BILLS-116hr5087ih.pdf (Accessed: 5 May 2021).

US Congress, House (2020) *Testimony of Heath Burleson, Partnership Advisor, Corvias Group.* Available at: congress.gov/116/meeting/house/110611/witnesses/HHRG-116-AP18-Wstate-BurlesonM-20200303.pdf (Accessed: 5 May 2021).

US Congress, Senate (2001) 'S.842-US Public Safety Act'. 107th Congress, 1st Session. Available at: congress.gov/107/bills/s842/BILLS-107s842is.pdf (Accessed: 20 January 2020).

US Congress, Senate (2018) *Hearing To Receive Testimony on the Current Condition of the Military Housing Privatization Initiative.* Available at: https://www.armed-services.senate.gov/hearings/19-02-13-current-condition-of-the-military-housing-privatization-initiative (Accessed: 20 March 2020).

US Department of Defense (2016) *Department of Defense Real Property Portfolio.* Office of the Assistant Secretary of Defense for Sustainment. Available at: acq.osd.mil/eie/Downloads/Fast_Facts_2016.pdf (Accessed: 3 March 2019).

US Department of Defense (n.d.) *Real Property, Office of the Assistant Secretary of Defense for Sustainment.* Available at: https://www.acq.osd.mil/eie/bsi/bei_rpa.html (Accessed: 3 March 2019).

US Department of Defense, Office of the Inspector General (2015a) *Continental United States Military Housing Inspections – National Capital Region.* DODIG-2015–162. Available at: https://www.dodig.mil/reports.html/Article/1119195/continental-united-states-military-housing-inspection-national-capital-region/ (Accessed: 20 June 2018).

US Department of Defense, Office of the Inspector General (2015b) *Continental United States Military Housing Inspections-Southeast.* DODIG-2015–181. Available at: https://www.dodig.mil/reports.html/Article/1119209/continental-united-states-military-housing-inspections-southeast/ (Accessed: 20 June 2019).

US Department of Defense, Office of the Inspector General (2016) *Summary Report – Inspections of DoD Facilities and Military Housing and Audits of Base Operations and Support Services Contracts.* DODIG-2017–004. Available at: https://www.dodig.mil/reports.html/Article/1119324/summary-report-inspections-of-dod-facilities-and-military-housing-and-audits-of/ (Accessed: 2 August 2019).

US Department of Education, Office of the Inspector General (2016) *Nationwide Assessment of Charter and Education Management Organizations.* ED-OIGA02M0012. Available at:

https://www.oversight.gov/report/ed/nationwide-assessment-charter-and-education-man
agement-organizations (Accessed: 3 March 2020).

US Department of Education, Office of the Inspector General (2018) *Nationwide Audit of Oversight of Closed Charter.* ED-OIGA02M0011. Available at: https://www.oversight.gov/ report/ed/nationwide-audit-oversight-closed-charter (Accessed: 2 February 2020).

US Department of Education, Office of the Inspector General (2019) *IDEA Public Schools' Administration of Grants for the Replication and Expansion of High-Quality Charter Schools.* ED-OIG/A05S0013. Available at: https://www.oversight.gov/report/ed/idea-pub lic-schools%E2%80%99-administration-grants-replication-and-expansion-high-quality-charter (Accessed: 20 February 2020).

US Department of Homeland Security, Office of the Inspector General (2018) *ICE's Inspections and Monitoring of Detention Facilities Do Not Lead to Sustained Compliance or Systemic Improvements.* OIG-18 – 67. Available at: oig.dhs.gov/sites/default/files/assets/ 2018 – 06/OIG-18 – 67-Jun18.pdf (Accessed: 19 February 2019).

US Department of Homeland Security, Office of the Inspector General (2019) *Concerns About ICE Detainee Treatment and Care at Four Detention Facilities.* OIG-19 – 47. Available at: oig.dhs.gov/sites/default/files/assets/2019 – 06/OIG-19 – 47-Jun19.pdf (Accessed: 20 February 2020).

US Department of Justice, Office of the Inspector General (2016) *Review of the Federal Bureau of Prisons' Monitoring of Contract Prisons.* Evaluations and Inspections Division 16 – 06. Available at: https://www.oversight.gov/sites/default/files/oig-reports/e1606.pdf (Accessed: 3 March 2019).

US Department of the Army, Office of the Inspector General (2019) *Special Interest Item Assessment of the Residential Communities Initiative (RCI).* Report ID-1903. Available at: https://www.army.mil/e2/downloads/rv7/families/releaseable-housing-inspection.pdf (Accessed: 20 January 2020).

US Deputy Secretary of Defense (1998) 'Privatizing Utility Systems, Memorandum'. Available at: https://archive.defense.gov/dodreform/drids/drid49.html (Accessed: 4 January 2020).

US Government Accountability Office (2005) *Defense Infrastructure: Management Issue Requiring Attention in Utility Privatization.* Report GAO-05 – 433. Available at: https://digi tal.library.unt.edu/ark:/67531/metadc301313/ (Accessed: 3 January 2020).

US Government Accountability Office (2010) 'Memo To Congressional Committees'. Available at: gao.gov/new.items/d10725r.pdf (Accessed: 3 January 2020).

US Government Accountability Office (2013) *Human Capital: Additional Steps Needed to Help Determine the Right Size and Composition of DOD's Total Workforce.* GAO-13 – 470. Available at: https://www.gao.gov/products/gao-13-470 (Accessed: 20 January 2020).

US Government Accountability Office (2018a) *Defense Infrastructure: Guidance Needed to Develop Metrics and Implement Cybersecurity Requirements for Utilities Privatization Contracts.* GAO-18 – 558. Available at: https://www.gao.gov/products/gao-18-558 (Accessed: 8 February 2020).

US Government Accountability Office (2018b) *Military Housing Privatization: DOD Should Take Steps to Improve Monitoring, Reporting, and Risk Assessment.* GAO-18 – 218. Available at: https://www.gao.gov/products/gao-18-218 (Accessed: 2 August 2020).

US Securities and Exchange Commission (2012) *The GEO Group, Inc.* Annual Report 1 – 14260. Washington, DC. Available at: https://www.sec.gov/Archives/edgar/data/923796/ 000119312513087892/d493925d10k.htm (Accessed: 1 January 2020).

Van Heertum, R. and Alberto Torres, C. (2012) 'Educational Reform in the U.S. in the Past 30 Years: Great Expectations and the Fading American Dream', in Olmos, L., Alberto Torres, C., and Van Heertum, R. (eds) *Educating the Global Citizen: In the Shadow of Neoliberalism Thirty Years of Educational Reform in North America*. Potoma, MD: Bentham Science Publishers, pp. 3–27. doi: 10.2174/9781608052684111101010003.

Vick, K. (2009) 'As "Rescissions" Spawn Outrage, Health Insurers Cite Fraud Control', *Washington Post*, 8 September. Available at: https://www.washingtonpost.com/wp-dyn/con tent/article/2009/09/07/AR2009090702455.html?noredirect=on (Accessed: 21 June 2017).

Vine, D. (2014) '"We're Profiteers": How Military Contractors Reap Billions from U.S. Military Bases Overseas', *Monthly Review*, pp. 82–102. doi: 10.14452/MR-066–03–2014–07_6.

Vine, D. (2017) 'The Costs and Benefits of US Bases Overseas'. Available at: talkmedianews.com/world-news/2017/05/01/wake-costs-benefits-us-overseas-bases/ (Accessed: 2 January 2020).

Volsky, I. (2014) 'Obama Makes Surprise Reversal On Obamacare', *ThinkProgress*, 8 April. Available at: https://archive.thinkprogress.org/obama-makes-surprise-reversal-on-obama care-f8214392f8d2/ (Accessed: 3 May 2020).

Wacquant, L. (2001) 'Deadly Symbiosis: When Ghetto and Prison Meet and Mesh', *Punishment & Society*, 3(1), pp. 95–133. doi: 10.1177/14624740122228276.

Wagner, P. and Rabuy, B. (2017) *Following the Money of Mass Incarceration*. Prison Policy Initiative. Available at: https://www.prisonpolicy.org/reports/money.html (Accessed: 5 May 2021).

Wagner, P. and Sawyer, W. (2020) *Mass Incarceration: The Whole Pie 2020*. Prison Policy Initiative. Available at: https://www.prisonpolicy.org/reports/pie2020.html (Accessed: 1 May 2020).

Waitzkin, H. and Hellander, I. (2016) 'Obamacare: The Neoliberal Model Comes Home to Roost in the United States—If We Let It', *Monthly Review*, 68(1), p. 1. doi: 10.14452/MR-068–01–2016–05_1.

White, W., Pena, A. A. and Weiler, S. (2020) 'Going private: Are private prisons cost-saving options for states?', *Growth and Change*, 51(3), pp. 1000–1016. doi: 10.1111/grow.12388.

Wilkins, B. (2021) *With California Single-Payer Bill Shelved, Advocates Call on Newsom to Take Lead on Medicare for All*. Common Dreams. Available at: https://www.common dreams.org/news/2021/04/23/california-single-payer-bill-shelved-advocates-call-news om-take-lead-medicare-all (Accessed: 3 May 2021).

Wood, E. (1992) *The pristine culture of capitalism: a historical essay on old regimes and modern states*. London: Verso.

Wood, E. (2002) *Empire of Capital*. London: Verso.

Wood, N. (2004) *Tyranny in America: capitalism and national decay*. London: Verso.

Zenko, M. (2016) 'Mercenaries Are the Silent Majority of Obama's Military', *Foreign Policy*, 18 May. Available at: https://foreignpolicy.com/2016/05/18/private-contractors-are-the-silent-majority-of-obamas-military-mercenaries-iraq-afghanistan/ (Accessed: 3 January 2020).

Zion Market Research (2018) *U.S. Education Market Will Reach USD 2,040 billion by 2026: Zion Market Research*. GlobeNewswire. Available at: https://www.globenewswire.com/news-release/2018/04/09/1466926/0/en/U-S-Education-Market-Will-Reach-USD-2-040-billion-by-2026-Zion-Market-Research.html (Accessed: 12 January 2020).

Index

ww.ingramcontent.com/pod-product-compliance